Social Science Frontiers

Occasional Publications Reviewing New Fields
for Social Science Development

**Work and Family in the United States:
A Critical Review and Agenda
for Research and Policy**

By Rosabeth Moss Kanter

Russell Sage Foundation

1977

Russell Sage Foundation
230 Park Avenue
New York, N.Y. 10017

Library of Congress Catalog Number: 76-46870
ISBN: 0-87154-433-4
Third Printing, 1979

Contents

Introduction

This report explores the development of a social science frontier: theory, research, and policy concerning the dynamic intersections of work and family systems in contemporary American society. The impetus for effort on work-family interactions comes from several sources. In their concern for the increased well-being of citizens, national policy makers have recently focused attention on the impact of the structure and availability of work for the quality of life (see O'Toole, 1974). At the same time, Walter Mondale in the Senate, and others have turned attention to dilemmas and changes in family structure, arguing for the creation of a national family policy which would, in turn, consider the effects on family life of governmental legislation and organizational decisions. The Foundation for Child Development, for example, has recently supported an investigation of the feasibility of attaching "family impact" statements to legislation.

Such concerns derive from specific social changes as well as a general interest in the quality of life. The women's movement and the increase of women in the paid labor force (especially married women with children) have focused policy attention on the work-family link for women: the extent to which work systems make it possible to maintain effective participation in both worlds. A rise in the number of single-parent families has similarly directed attention to the question of bridging the two worlds. And these issues, of course, are of critical interest to those individuals who find themselves bearing major responsibilities in both domains (working mothers or single-parent fathers). The 1960s also brought a number of social movements challenging the usual patterns of middle-class work and family life. Concerns with some unfortunate human effects of contemporary economic organization (pollution, executive ulcers, etc.) and the "growth potential" inherent in private life led to a variety of experiments (communes, work cooperatives) in which people tried to connect work and private life in very different ways, giving priority to leisure, personal expression, and relationships rather than career mobility. The movements of the past decade gave rise to the common use of the term *life-style* and awareness of the plurality of life-styles in the society (Zablocki and Kanter, 1976). There has also been a growing awareness of a turning away from career striving as the dominant measure of individual success, along with a revaluing of private, family life on the part of professionals inside organizations (Bailyn and Schein, 1976) as well as younger people (Gartner and Reissman, 1974), particularly as the personal "costs" of overly work-absorbed careers have been made clear. And studies of work and leisure, especially in the late 1950s and early 1960s, began to focus attention on this critical link (e.g., Riesman, 1958; Wilensky, 1961).

Several recent intellectual trends have also highlighted the importance of studying work and family life together. In sociology and economics, a revival of interest in Marxist theory and research has taken a first premise that no part of modern life goes uninfluenced by the structure of capitalist institutions. Families as well as schools, in this view, take their own shape from the demands of capitalism for workers and consumers (Bowles and Gintis, 1976). Thus, the family is one of the critical links in the capitalist economy, as it both produces "labor power" and consumes goods and services. Secondly, in psychology, sociology, and psychohistory, a concern with the total life cycle has also led to interest in the variety of settings in which adults as well as children spend their lives as both family members and workers. A growing interest in adult development naturally leads to questions about the ways in which people are shaped by and manage their multiple involvements in their private as well as organizational lives. The timing of events in both the work and family worlds has also begun to receive attention in this developmental perspective (Brim and Abeles, 1975; Rapoport and Rapoport, 1965). (Hareven, 1974, has argued that historical studies of family structure also need to add this developmental focus on the family as "process," unfolding and changing over the life cycle.) Developments in certain applied fields also pave the way for the examination of work-family linkages. In both organizational social psychology (applied behavioral science or industrial psychology) and the growing field of family therapy, open systems theory has provided a useful perspective. Organization development has concerned itself with integrating social and technical aspects of work, and family therapy has taken as its central premise the notion that the problems of individuals must be seen and treated in the context of the total family system (e.g., Kantor and Lehr, 1975). The open systems perspective (see Katz and Kahn, 1966) makes it possible to consider the inputs into each system from others in its environment.

Finally, the evolving character of the society as a whole has made this a particularly good time to consider the relations of work and family life. Growth in the numbers of people employed in service institutions and other changes signalling the "post-industrial society" have led scholars, such as Daniel Bell (1973), to conclude that in the future economic enterprises will pay more attention to their "sociologizing" (i.e., human welfare) functions than their "economizing" (profit-making) functions. But, of course, people come to work in organizations not just as individuals but also as members of private systems, such as families, that are themselves affected by the policies and practices of organizations. It may be that organizations of the future will have to pay attention to their effects on people other than employed persons (spouses, children) and allow the needs of families to influence organizational decisions and shape organizational policies. Questions about day care, part-time work, maternity and paternity leave, executive transfers, spousal involvement in career planning, and treatment of family dysfunctions—all difficult to approach at present—may become primary considerations for organizations in the future.

For all of these reasons, then, it is important to raise and consider the nature and problems of work-family connections for people in a variety of social circumstances. This report attempts to offer some of the relevant background, by synthesizing previous studies and providing a coherent framework for current reflection. It is intended to raise questions that can provide an impetus to further investigation, to outline directions for fruitful exploration. There are several possible audiences: social science researchers, primarily in sociology and psychology; individual practitioners in mental health and human welfare fields; legislators and other social policy formulators; and internal staff and decision makers in work organizations, particularly large employers.

I begin with some historical and sociological speculation about why the gap between work and family has been maintained in the contemporary United States, locating some tentative answers both in industrial-organizational history and in the sociology of social science. The changes noted earlier are already helping to bridge the gap. The second section deals with the impact of occupational structures and work organization on families, identifying five dimensions or aspects of work positions that bear on family relations: the degree of occupational "absorption"; time and timing; the provision of rewards, both material and symbolic; occupational and organizational culture; and emotional aspects of one's structural location at work. But individuals and families are not merely passive recipients of occupational and economic influences. Thus, the third section examines the family as an independent variable: a number of ways in which families and family life influence work decisions and the world of work. Because most of the research in these areas has dealt with the man as worker and breadwinner, and because women have traditionally faced a different situation as workers, the fourth section deals separately with women's employment and family relations. It considers some issues around non-market work (home or housework) as well as work in the paid labor market, and it notes especially those changes in our models and methods required by a more realistic and nontraditional picture of women. Women bring work influences into the family as well as personal needs into work situations. The fifth section moves from those social structural considerations that can be more easily quantified into a social psychological frontier: qualitative exploration of working and loving as processes. Here the concern is with modes of interaction and the degree of convergence between

4

task-oriented and intimate relationships. In the sixth section, views of the effects of both work life and family life on personal well-being are raised, and it is suggested that the joint effects of the two systems be considered simultaneously, since the impact either sector has on the other depends heavily on the nature of the second system itself. How work pressures and stresses affect an individual and his or her family, for example, depends critically on the kind of family system in operation, just as the effect of family stresses on work life depends on the human organization of the work setting. Questions and issues for further research and policy consideration are raised throughout the discussion, but the last section summarizes major items for a research and policy agenda.

This review touches a large number of bases, but it inevitably leaves out some matters of importance. There is a stream in economics dealing with the decisions of individuals to allocate their time and resources across work and family systems, as well as a large number of writings on the family as an economic unit; these areas are not mentioned. I also do not review the large sociological literature on social mobility, in which the relative importance of family background for occupational, educational, or income attainments is extensively researched. Macro-social studies of the structure of the family under various stages of industrialization are left out, and demographic issues, such as fertility, family size, or relative age at marriage, are not considered. Such areas are all very important and well worth the attention of researchers. But they are not necessarily "frontiers," because strong research traditions are already established.

A note on language and scope: the term *work* is often used synonymously with *paid employment,* for the sake of convenience, even though I recognize that *work* has a much broader meaning and legitimately encompasses non-market work, such as housework and volunteer work. At times in this report I do consider the effects of the organization of such non-market activities, especially in section four. And I would argue that to the extent that non-market work is as demanding and absorbing as market work, it can be analyzed using the same dimensions outlined in section two. Similarly, the term *family* is never really defined in the paper, since there are useful discussions elsewhere of the multiple meanings and confusing usages of the concept (e.g., Skolnick, 1975). *Family* tends to mean here the sphere of intimate others, usually co-residents in the household, but also networks of kin outside; the fact that most often effects on marital bonds or on parent-child relationships are stressed is a function of the major emphases in the literature I review and not my personal preference. The realm of the family, similarly, encompasses here, for convenience, leisure pursuits and non-market work activities, even though these may sometimes be done by individuals with or without the participation of their "families." Thus, the issue of family boundaries is not directly addressed, and I try to make few *a priori* assumptions about the appropriate unit in which particular work effects on personal life manifest themselves. But I am sure that not all unconscious biases have been exorcised, despite considerable care. The explicit limitation of scope to the United States (although I review a few studies based on other English-speaking countries) is a reflection of my attempt not to generalize beyond my own area of cultural familiarity. But, hopefully, this report will have broader usefulness.

I am grateful to Russell Sage Foundation for supporting this effort, especially Hugh Cline, under whose leadership this report was undertaken, Sarane Boocock, who provided intelligent advice and encouragement, and Jean Yoder, who shepherded the manuscript into publication. Valuable comments were provided by Jessie Bernard, Andrew Cherlin, Frank Furstenberg, Robert Rapoport, and Barry Stein, as well as several anonymous reviewers; Rapoport wrote particularly extensive comments. Susan Bell and Rosanna Hertz provided helpful library research, and Report Production Associates, Vivian Kaufman, and the Brandeis Sociology Department office staff assisted with the typing. Some of the work for this paper was carried out during 1975-76, when I held a Guggenheim Fellowship and was in residence at Harvard Law School; thanks are therefore also due to the John Simon Guggenheim Foundation.

How the Gap Grew:
Some Historical and Sociological Speculations

Contemporary social scientists tend to agree: a strong link exists between economic variables and family life. Critical to the traditional sociological definition of the modern family is the family's "loss" of productive functions with the Industrial Revolution, but its continued economic importance as a consumption unit. Consumption in a monetized economy requires money income, so that the patterns families establish are closely tied to the financial conditions of earners, traditionally viewed in terms of the occupational prospects of husband-fathers. Consumption style and the prestige accorded to families in their community (termed *status* by Max Weber and assumed to devolve on families as a unit) are further mediated by the nature of occupations themselves and their relation to systems of production (*class* in the Marxist and Weberian senses). Whether work is manual or nonmanual, to use one common distinction, affects both class and status, as well as bringing with it a set of life chances and life experiences that shape family and consumption decisions.

Yet, despite the agreement that the family and the economy as institutions are linked in *broad* ways, the specific intersections

7

and transactions between work and family, between occupations and families as connected organizers of experience and systems of social relations, are virtually ignored. There are only a handful of studies that consider the connections between forms of work and family life (as opposed to general social class and family variables). Even structuralist analyses of the impact of economic location on life-style rarely employ differentiated occupational categories or consider the structure of particular occupations as constraints for family choices. (Exceptions are reviewed on pp. 23-51.) And there is only a limited amount of research or theory that considers the behavior and experiences of people in both their work and family situations by looking at people in both contexts. This conclusion was reached after a review of several hundred articles and books. What is the gap, and why does it exist?

The Myth of Separate Worlds

If any one statement can be said to define the most prevalent sociological position on work and family, it is the "myth" of separate worlds. The myth goes like this: In a modern industrial society work life and family life constitute two separate and non-overlapping worlds, with their own functions, territories, and behavioral rules. Each operates by its own laws and can be studied independently. If events or decisions in one world (such as the wages awarded a worker) enter the other, they enter in the guise of external (and hence, often extraneous) variables but are not an intrinsic part of the operation of that world. They help shape a context, but little more. Few contemporary industrial analysts would deny that sophisticated analysis of an organization ought to take into account the composition of its work force, including family status and sex (with its implied family position). Nor would enlightened family sociologists fail to take into account social class, grossly measured by income level and occupational status, in understanding family systems. But neither group is at all likely to consider the operation of the world studied by the other or to look for dynamic connections between them.

"A myth," Sebastian de Grazia has reminded us, "is not a lie. It is something almost everyone wants to believe. In believing it, he sometimes embraces a cold [finding] too warmly" (de Grazia, 1962:63). The myth of separate worlds is not without truth, then,

8

but it is far from all of the picture. How this image developed and has been sustained is an important question in itself. Indeed, it is revealing to examine why we *have not* studied more work-family intersections and transactions, before suggesting what we ought to be studying. Some speculation based on social theory and recent historical research follows; further research can be developed to test and refine the argument.

Nepotism and Anti-nepotism: The Historical Backdrop

Historically and cross-culturally, organizations of all kinds that want to exact loyalty and commitment from members, especially those making a radical break with the past, attempt to exclude or neutralize particularistic ties that might compete with loyalty to the system as a whole (Kanter, 1968, 1972a; Coser, 1975). The family is an especially insidious source of particularistic loyalties. For one thing, it combines both sexuality and authority. Sexuality has for a long time been considered the enemy of work discipline; Freud incorporated it into an overarching theory of the tensions between sexual instincts and civilization (Freud, 1962). But the authority relations represented in the traditional institution of family are equally threatening to organizations for which authority is the *sine qua non* of existence. The authority of parents over children, husbands (in the traditional model) over wives, and in even more traditional systems, elder kin over younger ones—all might compete with the authority of the organization. The fact that family members choose one another (in the case of marriage) or find themselves together (in the case of birth) for reasons totally unconnected with the organization's purposes further threatens to undercut its authority, if it begins to lose control over selection. Furthermore, within larger systems the family can easily form a natural coalition. Family members might band together as a political force, might favor one another in decisions on grounds far removed from the organization's purposes or interests, and might exclude fellow worker-members from organizationally relevant deliberations, because of the family's right to withdraw privately to its own quarters. Indeed, Weber (1947:354-8) felt that strong family influences could undermine the development of rational bureaucracies based on individual merit (Rapoport, 1975a).

9

The dilemma for a loyalty-demanding organization, then, is this: whether to try to incorporate and thus co-opt the family into serving the organization's ends, or whether to try to exclude it by replacing its functions or placing them clearly outside the boundaries of the workplace. Recent histories of the family's relation to the evolving capitalist-industrial system seem to indicate that the family was first incorporated into organization life and then pushed outside.

The Industrial Revolution began to make organization membership (and a dependent form of membership, at that) a factor in more and more productive work, even though it took many decades for the modern system of large organizations with professional managers to evolve. The issue of particularistic ties and what to do about the family was brought to a head with the transfer of work from family enterprises to larger, more impersonal organizations and with the development of systems of management (Nelson, 1975; see also Kanter, 1977: Chapter 1; Braverman, 1974). Families and their rootedness to particular places represented a major source of resistance to early British industrialization, and employers were often forced to import foreign labor in order to find workers willing to submit to organizational authority and discipline (de Grazia, 1962: 185-6).

But at the same time, in the first few decades of the nineteenth century, the family was an important work unit in city factories in England, as it was nearly a century later in New England (Hareven, 1975a, 1975b). Spinners in textile mills chose their wives, children, and near relatives as assistants, generally paying them from their own wages. Children entering the factory at eight or nine worked for their fathers, perpetuating the old system of authority and the traditional values of parents training children for occupations. In the 1820s and 1830s this system began to decline, partly to undermine the traditional economic authority of spinners (Smelser, 1959: 189-90, 198). Familial influences and ties in early industrial organizations seem to have been maintained much longer in the United States, as shown in Hareven's extensive historical research on Manchester, New Hampshire, and the Amoskeag Corporation. Indeed, she argues against sociological tradition in asserting that it was the family system that made possible the transition from preindustrial to industrial ways of life (1975b). (See also Gutman, 1973, on the transition.) Before the adoption of modern management systems,

10

which were developed largely between 1890 and World War I, the family often functioned as a labor recruiter, a housing agent, an influence on the job placement of its members, and even a unit which could affect daily job control (Hareven, 1975a:372). Before personnel and recruitment systems were devised, organizations often relied on workers to bring in members of their families, and this was a large source of new women employees in factories during World War I (Nelson, 1975:145). But the degree to which the family could exercise some control over and within the workplace was very much a function of ethnic group and industry (contrast Hareven on textiles or Nelson on machinery shops with Byington, 1909, on steel).

Eventually, action against nepotism was taken, in order to extend control of managers over formerly more independent workers. In factories, at least, the unformed (children) or the unattached (young unmarried women) were often the preferred workers, because of the assumption of their greater malleability. The nineteenth-century textile mills of Connecticut, Rhode Island, and southern Massachusetts replaced the "family system," in which whole families were employed and wages and tasks assigned by age and sex, with a "boarding house system," devised by Boston financiers, that employed young unmarried women from rural areas as temporary workers and housed them in company facilities (Vogel, 1975).

Such systems were eventually ended by child labor laws protecting children from exploitation and other protective legislation for women. But by then, de Grazia has pointed out, factory owners had managed to train a generation in appropriate work habits and thus to create its labor force (1963:188). Organizations at this time, primarily the capitalist proprietors— found it to be in their interest to break the family's control over work and workers, and this was an important consequence of the movement toward systematic or scientific management (Nelson, 1975). (Japan, of course, handled the problem differently.)

Other attempts to cope with the family problem in early industrialization involved swallowing the family and taking over its functions. One move was to make workplaces into "total institutions" in the form of company towns and company lodging. (See Nelson, 1975:90-95, 102-6.) Some independence was lost to the family in such settings, and the organization had access to

11

the private or nonworking aspects of workers' lives. Corporate "welfare" programs at the turn of the century, such as those of the H. J. Heinz Co. of Pittsburgh in the 1880s and 1890s or the kindergartens run by National Cash Register in Dayton, often employed the imagery of the company as a "family," and in some cases there were intrusions into workers' homes—inspections to see if they were living respectable lives (Nelson, 1975:102, 108, 150). This "solution" was never widely accepted, although there are still textile mills in the south where integration of the family extends organizational control over workers (Bluner, 1964:77). It eventually raised questions about totalistic control, and it kept the family as a work-relevant unit, giving it a basis for joint resistance or influence. Nor did such takeovers of the family continue to be necessary with the growth of cities, schools, and an organization-habituated labor force. Instead, anti-nepotism rules, prohibiting the employment of close family members (usually husbands and wives) tended to hold sway (Caplow, 1954:237). They are only today beginning to undergo change, as couple job-sharing, co-worker marriage, and hiring relatives become more possible ("Marrying . . . ," 1975). (The history of anti-nepotism rules in the context of modern organizations would be a valuable study.)*

Schools, especially, sided with other organizations in their war against particularism and their desire to fit workers to the workplace. Seeking discipline and wanting to legitimate their own authority claims, schools removed children from the family, set up a system of authority based on state sanction and expertise (grounds with which few parents, especially the large American immigrant population, could compete), and instituted a "work" discipline strikingly similar to that of adult organizations (Katz, 1968, 1971; Kanter, 1972b; Bowles and Gintis, 1976; the latter, especially, provide fine historical documentation for this argument). Today the relations between schools and parents and between teachers and parents, despite alleged community control

---

*Organizations often identify their concern for the best interests of families as the reason for anti-nepotism rules. University officials, for example, in explaining why they prefer not to hire husbands and wives, may point to their concern for sparing embarrassment to a family if one member but not another is granted tenure, along with the awkwardness for the organization itself. But the reasons I have indicated seem more compelling. They explain a wide variety of actions against family ties within organizations of many kinds and in many historical periods (e.g., Kanter, 1972a: Chapter 4).

of schools, are not unlike the uneasy relation of corporations and families, with the family often unable to intervene in or influence organizational policies, even though these policies have great effects on their lives (Lightfoot, 1977).

As the development of industrial capitalism led to larger firms, as the available (and properly socialized) labor force increased, and as much work became less craft-like and more machine-like, creating work rhythms with their own high demand value, it is possible to argue that the need for loyalty from workers, with the concomitant tensions with the family, decreased. Production workers were no longer particularly independent. The family no longer entered the system of production, and workers were highly replaceable. Nepotism and distancing from the family was much less an issue on this level than for the white-collar, managerial, and professional classes. But it is not that organizations did not want to believe in the loyalty of their workers anyway; the idea of the committed worker whose major life interest is the company was a prevalent notion through the 1930s and 1940s. Perhaps the eagerness of the human-relations-industry school to "see" the strength of interpersonal involvements among workers, despite Robert Dubin's later report that relations at work are *not* that important to workers (1956), was a reflection of the desire to push away the family in support of the myth of separate worlds. The use of the very word "family" to refer to organizational work groups is revealing. Titmuss criticized the human relations in industry movement for just this blind spot:

> The factory or office comes to be seen as a complete, closed, autonomous system, pursuing its own goals and developing its own values and norms of behaviour regardless of the outside world. Seldom are the workers' activities and aspirations outside the factory considered. Rarely, if ever, are his family relationships and his place in the community discussed. (1969:110-11.)

For the white-collar classes, the growth pattern of cities also helped separate the family. Because industrialization was not a pleasant process, an ideology of home and hearth as the preserve of tradition and humanity grew through the nineteenth century —what Jeffrey (1972) has called the "home as utopian retreat from the city." Those who could afford to remove their residences to "pastoral" surroundings far from places of employment often did so, also removing, in the process, points of contact between

13

the rest of the family and the organization. (If the family realm represented a retreat from the urban-industrial jungle, however, the separate workplace also represented for men a possible retreat from intimacy, as it may continue to do today for some people.) It was the well-paid people—the least replaceable, with the most control over the organization's resources—whose loyalty, and hence freedom from particularistic ties, organizations needed most. And it was these same workers who perhaps tended to have the strongest degree of work-family territorial separation.

Territorial separation between residential and commercial/industrial districts, reinforced in the twentieth century by the advent of zoning and by striking architectural differences (until office buildings and high-rise apartments became indistinguishable), confirmed the tendency to see work and family as entirely separate. It is the middle-class family, after all, upon which many society-wide images of America are based, and suburbia has in many ways become the American version of "traditional society." (See Berger, 1960.) It is hardly surprising to notice, as the Crestwood Heights researchers did (Seeley, Sim, and Loosley, 1956), that for much of the time suburbia is populated only by women and children, the people who transform an individual worker into a "family" with "family life," and the man is plugged in when he appears, but *not* seen as carrying with him family membership when he goes off to work. (Working women *are* seen as always carrying a family, however, I will note later.) That the activities and attitudes of only women could be studied as constituting family life reinforced the myth of separate worlds and led some critics to conclude that we had "his" and "hers" marriages or a "wives' family sociology" rather than a "family sociology" (Bernard, 1972).

Separation of the occupational and family sectors of society came to be considered, by modern Parsonian theory as well as conventional wisdom of the post-World War II period, essential to the smooth functioning of each institution and thus to the integration of society as a whole. This view rested, first, on a definition of the norms of each sector as "incompatible." Occupational life in this perspective is organized around impersonal and objective standards of competence linked to the technical content of a function. These norms are directly opposed, Parsons (1949) argued, to those of the family, which instead rest on custom and particularistic and emotional

14

standards and define roles by age and sex categories rather than "objective" performance criteria. Parsons concluded that a strong separation of the two institutions permitted each to function with minimum interference from the conflicting standards of the other. The work world's interests were served in Parsonian theory, by making sure that only *one* member of a conjugal family unit played a "fully competitive" role in the occupational system and that workplaces were clearly distinct from residences. The family's interests were also served by this separation (and exclusion of married women from careers), for intimacy and solidarity can be retained, the theory held, only if husband, wife, and children do not engage in direct competition for prestige or rate performance by impersonal standards.

If other institutions, ideologies, and patterns facilitated the isolation of family ties from the world of organizations, it was still the organizations themselves that had the major stake in creating and preserving it. Capitalism and the growth of large work organizations only made "necessary" for more people a process of control of the family that other large loyalty-exacting organizations (such as the military and the Roman Catholic church) had also found supportive of an organization's power. But the vast majority of modern organizations are not total institutions, such as the priesthood or a monastery or a military base. They can do no more than push the family aside and exclude it from "business"; they cannot eliminate it completely. (Indeed, corporations at least began to put a premium on married men in management; presumably their "family responsibilities" made them less likely to behave uncooperatively or unpredictably and risk loss of promotion.) The compromise put into effect by the modern organization could be phrased as a dictate to members: "While you are here, you will *act as though* you have no other loyalties, no other life." (The demands made on key members, of course, reflect the consequences of this dictate.)

The "act as though" principle was reinforced by the myth of individual achievement: that people in American society rise or fall on their own. Thus the family as helper (a subject I will return to) could no more be taken into account than the family as a competing loyalty. Nor could the person-on-the-rise implicate his or her family (usually "his" because this is more allowable for women) without looking like something less honorific than the independent achiever.

15

If the territories of the organization and the family remain separate (as they do for large employers but *not* for many small businesses and family proprietorships), and if the only people to move physically between the two are directed to "act as though . . . ," then it is not surprising that attempts by researchers to discover connections between work and family by asking people about them directly might result in denials and refusals.

Denial of Connections

The myth of separate worlds is especially prevalent among certain occupational groups whose organizations have a stake in perpetuating it and who hold values of meritocratic individual achievement. These include managers and professionals, as well as academic researchers.* In the 1950s Aberle and Naegle (1952), among the few early researchers to ask people directly how their occupation affected their behavior in the family, interviewed twenty fathers (professionals, executives, and salesmen) and mothers of nursery school children. The fathers split into three camps. One group found only very trivial connections between their work and family behavior, one could not find *any*, and a third set firmly rejected the idea that there were any. (The persistent researchers managed to tease out only one work-family connection: that adults' occupational experiences shape their judgments about what qualities their children will need to succeed.) Another researcher came to a similar conclusion about denial: "Some men choose to deny any connection between their work and their family life, but research data indicate that their families display a keen perception of the work situation as it affects the father and the family" (Dyer, 1964:86).

Even recent studies, in a climate of greater awareness of the spillover effects from work to private life, have found the same sorts of denials. One example is illustrative. A UCLA graduate student in management, interested in the intersections of work and family, approached several companies looking for a site for her research (Renshaw, 1974). She was turned down because managers could see no relevant connections (or wanted to see

*Indeed, it is interesting to note that the description of the geographically mobile isolated nuclear family firmly detached from a workplace probably matches the situation of academic sociologists, even though it has been found wanting as a picture of most American families.

16

none). The site she finally found considered her research appropriate because the system was having problems: e.g., family strains translated into work strains because of executive travel or transfer. (Rapoport, 1975b, has pointed out that before the 1960s, the influence of work on family was studied only under such exceptional problem conditions, as when a man's family problems intruded themselves on the workplace, or vice versa, as in Whyte's, 1951, 1952, "wife of the organization man" studies.) Renshaw's open-ended interviews led her to see that, at least in her managerial sample, people indeed obscure the connections between work and family. Either they systematically deny, even to themselves, the connections between events and feelings occurring in the two different worlds; or, they "use" events in one world as "excuses" for feelings, behaviors, or inadequacies in the other, in a simplistic, rationalizing way. Renshaw concluded that people are simultaneously members of at least two systems, but while they are in one they often act and present themselves as though they had no other memberships. This manner of self-presentation and self-identification is, of course, congruent with organizational norms and the "act as though" principle I have identified.

I am arguing that there is a "fit" between the interests of modern American organizations, as they have developed in the context of American society, and the myth of separate worlds. If early corporations tried to swallow up the family in paternalistic company towns and welfare programs, modern ones tend to disclaim any responsibility for family lives of members. And social scientists as well as organization officials have often treated people in one world as though they have no connections with another. Consideration of linkages between work and family systems has generally been confined to analysis of how the quantity or type of "output" from one system (such as money or prestige from the work world or labor power from the family) enter into the operations of the other. So, historical-ideological reasons for the myth of separate worlds are compounded by the neglect of social science to close the gap. Some explanations for the lack of attention to work-family intersections may lie in traditional emphases of social science disciplines themselves, which are only now undergoing revision.

17

Current interest in work and family comes from the variety of political, cultural, and intellectual sources identified in the Introduction. But several social science traditions have tended to militate against attention to this issue in the past.

1. SOCIOLOGY AS THE STUDY OF SEPARATE INSTITUTIONS. Sociology has come to be a field studying institutions, and sociologists tend to specialize in the study of one or more institutions, just as psychologists specialize in institutional branches. As Willmott presents it, "One of the consequences of specialization among sociologists has been that, though there are fairly established 'sociologies' of the family, of industry, and . . . of leisure, there has been little attempt to link them to each other" (1971:575). And Rapoport, "Social scientists . . . tend to use a model of industrial society that emphasizes specialisation of social institutions. . . . In the academic disciplines, the organic-differentiation model [derived from Durkheim] is seen in the segregation of family, educational, and other 'sector' branches of sociology and psychology from one another" (1975a:277).

Furthermore, the emphasis, by and large, has been on structure rather than process and on sets of activities as the basic unit, rather than individual lives across institutional areas. The combination of these tendencies militates against considering, in a processual way, the behaviors and events, the exchanges and transactions, that link institutions—that mediate between structures and behavior. Each institution tends to be studied separately, and when they are considered together, it is often merely to identify broad elements of social structure. Within the study of institutions, the family field, especially, suffers from this lack of emphasis on process. With few exceptions, the traditional emphasis was almost totally on roles and positions and forms or outcomes for the individual, with relatively little conceptualizing of the family as an *interacting system* until recently. This may affect the ability to see interactions across systems.

2. SOCIAL PSYCHOLOGY AS A LABORATORY DISCIPLINE. Social psychology is generally a field in which process is studied, so that dynamic links between systems could be made. Its subject matter, after all, is the individual as group member. But, as critics before

me have said, social psychology has generally avoided the real world and real-world interactions, focusing instead on what can be caricatured as "short-term interactions between college-age strangers under conditions of manipulation and mistrust." Social psychologists *have* studied groups within organizations, but they have mostly stayed away from the family. (Miller and Swanson are one notable set of exceptions, especially 1958.)

3. SOCIALIZATION AS A CHILDHOOD PHENOMENON. Despite some efforts to look at adult socialization (e.g., Brim, 1966; Becker, 1956), and an upsurge of interest in "adult development" today, the thrusts of psychology and sociology combined in the past to confine the idea of socialization to childhood. I do not mean to imply that there has been no attention paid to socialization *into* organizations and groups as adults. But there has been little sense of the way that long-term adult involvements may have strong impact on character and world view and therefore affect behavior in other realms. Occupations take up a major portion of people's time; they may have great impact as socializers—not just to the occupation itself or to an organization, but also with respect to other roles and relationships, as in the family. The evolution of family relations may have parallel (though I would hypothesize not as strong) socialization functions. In the case of occupations, there may be not only indirect socialization (through work relations and experiences) but also, for higher status occupations, direct educational training oriented toward behavior and opinion change. (While training programs themselves are often evaluated, their role as "adult socializers" is rarely considered.) But the traditional view of education and character development as occurring relatively early in the life cycle (and, in some cases, supposedly stopping when visible bodily maturation ends) has made it unlikely that later effects would be studied.

4. ACCEPTANCE OF ROLE THEORY. Even if one were inclined to consider adult experiences as important socializers, some other dominant perspectives make it unlikely that the impact of these socializing experiences from one setting to another will be investigated. These include both role theory and its variant dramaturgical views. The premise that roles are situationally determined and that, if situations making conflicting demands can be segregated, adults are capable of quite comfortably playing a

19

variety of roles, seems firmly entrenched. Goffman's dramaturgical notions imply that new parts and new costumes can be adopted continually with little impact on any other play, since the core self, to the extent there is one, lies deeper anyway. We change roles every day like we change clothes. The acceptance of the ability to play roles (and don't we have the evidence of our senses that this is so?) as well as of the similarities in behavior among those occupying similar positions have led to a lack of concern with the transfers between roles: how performance in one may affect, condition, or shape performance in another.

The notion of role *conflict* does have the potential for beginning to link systems. But in this area, the myth of separate worlds is invoked in a dramatic and revealing way. Since a corollary of the myth is the assumed separation of men's and women's domains, with the family woman's place, work-family role conflicts have been studied for *women* in paid employment but not for men, until very recently (and see studies noted on pp. 53-58). Men have traditionally been assumed to integrate all of their roles neatly, while employed women were seen as having a problem.

5. QUANTITATIVE EMPHASES ON STATES AND RATES—OR STATICS AND SNAPSHOTS. Much quantitative research on the family tends to look for associations between variables measured at only one point in time and often based on self-reports in surveys, with the nature of the intervening links left to speculation rather than direct measurement or observation. This has been mentioned before in critical appraisals of sociological studies. The concern is with level of a global variable (a state) and its association with the frequency of another variable (a rate), as in studies of association between occupational status and divorce rates in the population. Conclusions about associations are drawn in such studies (albeit statistically significant associations) when a large number of deviant cases remain to be explained, indicating that perhaps more theoretical attention should be paid to the appropriate differentiations between "states." Research on family variables as shaped by "social class" or "occupational status" is a case in point. As Duncan (1968) pointed out, the concept of class is often used in such a way that it means little more than the "imposition of more or less arbitrary intervals" on a scale of a status variable: "An incredible amount of paper and ink has been wasted in presenting factitious solutions for the artificial problem of where

20

'class boundaries' really belong" (Duncan, 1968: 694).

Most research on social class and family life, aside from a few first-rate ethnographic studies, consists of associational snapshots with measurement problems, such as those Duncan identified. But rarely are these important questions addressed: How is the large proportion of *overlap* between social "classes" in such studies to be explained? Have the most relevant occupational differentiations been made? What features of the process and dynamics of each situation account for the associations that do exist? How is *structure* (implied in a *state*) translated into *process* (implied in a *rate*)? What happens if occupational status *changes*, as it does for those workers who move between manual labor and starting their own small business (Mayer and Goldstein, 1964; Berg and Rogers, 1964)?

In the search for static quantitative associations, then, several important issues may be lost: theoretical significance, attention to mediating processes, and longitudinal (or cross-sectional) investigations of the modification of the relationship between states and rates over individual life cycles and historical time. Quantitative research can also benefit from considering more variables and more dynamic models, instead of remaining content with general associations. (Indeed, structural and processual issues of work influences on the family, as discussed in the following section, lend themselves to the building of quantitative models as well as more qualitative case analyses.)

Toward a Closing of the Gap

The myth of separate worlds certainly has some truth, but its accuracy itself varies with structural position in the society. Individual preference for separation or integration of work and family also plays a part. There are great differences in the degree of work-family connectedness even in advanced industrial society. And despite separate territories and an organizational image of "non-intrusion," the structure of work has a variety of strong influences on family life. Work operates as a dominant constraint on family life as well as a source of economic and personal sustenance.

21

The Dominant Influences:
Effects of the Structure of Occupations and the
Organization of Work on Family Life

The organization of work and the worker's position within it can have a variety of effects on family life. It is not occupational category and "class" level alone (or perhaps even primarily) that shape work-family interaction but rather a variety of issues stemming from the occupational milieu, the nature of the setting in which work occurs, and the location of work in organizational structures. The evidence reviewed on the following pages suggests the importance of taking a closer look at the occupational-organizational world than is usually done in stratification research in order to define more appropriate distinctions between types of work relations with differential effects on personal relations. As Wilensky pointed out:

it is clear that *class cultures* (sustained by similar levels of income and education and common absorption of the mass media) and *ethnic-religious cultures* (sustained by common descent and early socialization) significantly shape social relations. It is also clear that *occupational cultures* (rooted in common tasks, work schedules, job training, and career patterns) are sometimes better predictors of behavior than both social class and pre-job experience. (1961: 521-2.)

Wilensky is not alone in questioning the primacy of "class" in studies of the occupational world's effect on other societal

23

processes. Hatt had long argued for the importance of "situs," a horizontal dimension, in stratification research, saying that

> fertility differentials between physician and architect, electrician and plumber, accountant and clerk, may contain as valuable information as those differentials between physician, architect, and accountant on the one hand and plumber, electrician, and clerk on the other. (1950: 543.)

The many reports of findings about social class and life-style, for example, often use gross and oversimplified categories— sometimes as few as two—and do not make readily apparent both the great variation within classes and the overlap between them. Turner also commented that

> a careful re-examination of some of the prior studies of class differences in values shows that the relationships shown by others have often been quite modest. Frequently, only significance measures are reported, so that the low degree of relationship is not called to the attention of the reader. Often indexes composed of several items conceal the fact that some of the items are not themselves related to stratification. Second, several studies of childrearing patterns have revealed much less impressive class differences than were heretofore supposed to exist. (1964: 213.)

Finally, recent evidence and controversy about changes in stratification patterns, e.g., Goldthorpe et al., 1969 (Is the affluent working class becoming middle class? Are white-collar workers beginning to form a "new proletariat?" Is there an old and a new working class?) encourage a look beyond "class," as defined by census occupational categories, into the structure of work and the work experience itself. I also suggest that the notion of "social class" as a single continuum (e.g., an occupational prestige and income hierarchy) needs revision. Depending on economic position, either property, relative income, or occupation may be the most salient determinant of behavior and life-style. For the "upper classes" life-style and family relations may center around the ownership of property (real and symbolic) and the desire to ensure continuity of ownership with occupational category much less salient; the "lower classes" may find their lives dominated by income deprivation rather than specific job characteristics. But for the vast middle range of people who trade labor for wages or fees on the market, the structure of work and the constraints of occupations may be the most critical elements in shaping personal lives. (See Zablocki and Kanter, 1976, for extensions and consequences of this argument.)

Several aspects of the structure and organization of work life seem most important in shaping and influencing family systems, building on useful previous formulations (Gerstl, 1961; Rapoport and Rapoport, 1965; Parker, 1967; Aldous, 1969b). The first is the relative absorptiveness of an occupation—the extent to which it draws in and demands performance from other family members. The second is time and timing—the effects of work hours and schedules (daily, monthly, and yearly rhythms including the timing of major work history events). A consideration of time also helps generate a developmental perspective on work-family interactions (Rapoport and Rapoport, 1965). The third aspect is reward and resources—the "income" provided by occupations. Examined here is a more "economic" approach to family life in the exchange model along with some limitations of the model. The fourth aspect is world view, the culture dimension of work—occupations as socializers and teachers of values. Finally there is emotional climate, the social-psychological dimension of work—the personal experiencing of the world and of self offered by the work environment as a function of location in an organizational system. Some evidence and gaps in each of these areas will be considered.

Furstenberg, in reviewing material on family stability as a background paper for the Work in America investigations, commented that "the vast majority of sociological studies have used greatly simplified measures of the work status of individuals" (1974: 343). Attention to conceptualization of work experiences can generate finer, more sophisticated, and perhaps even more significant measures.

Absorption

Occupations differ in how much they absorb and subsume workers' lives; they fall along a continuum from highly salient and absorptive to minimally salient and non-absorptive. It was the existence of jobs at the low end of the continuum—those involving rather little of the person, performed for the pay involved, not constituting a "central life interest" for workers, and implicating little or none of their off-the-job life—that led Dubin (1956) to comment that social experience is inevitably segmented. For such workers work and family may indeed constitute highly separated, highly segregated worlds; each may

25

operate on its own terms, with the other acting only as an externality (in the economic sense) or a boundary-setting condition.

However, at the other end of the continuum in highly absorptive occupations, work and family may be so closely intertwined as to make it virtually impossible to consider one without considering the other. By *absorptive,* I mean occupational pursuits that not only demand the maximum commitment of the worker and define the context for family life; but also implicate other family members and command their direct participation in the work system in either its formal or informal aspects. Sometimes the occupation creates high identification in the worker (Becker and Carper, 1956) and demands activities that spill over beyond the work day, into "leisure" or private life, such as the press toward community involvement for executives (Levinson et al., 1962). Sometimes the nature of the occupation demands the participation of other family members, giving them job-related tasks to perform; sometimes it structures norms and role expectations for other family members. In any case, work effectiveness bears some relation to total family effort, and family life is dominated by work in absorptive occupations.

Relatively more absorptive occupations with clear job-related tasks for wives are more likely to be found at upper status levels among executives (Whyte, 1951, 1952; Warner and Abegglen, 1955, 1956; Steiner, 1972; Seidenberg, 1973; Kanter, 1977), foreign service officers (Hochschild, 1969), high-status politicians, the military (Goldman, 1973), and certain professions. Indeed, critics assert that in such fields the wife essentially has an unpaid career, a pattern Papanek (1973) called the "two-person single career." However, high absorptiveness can also be found in some less elite occupations: among farm families, proprietors of small restaurants or retail establishments, Peace Corps volunteers, and even teachers and police in small towns. In all such instances, the job defines tasks and performance standards for other family members. It is a major structural constraint on their activities and may even influence the extent to which the wife seeks a job on her own (Mortimer, Hall, and Hill, 1976). Some of these work pursuits may also involve physical arrangements that keep home and the workplace together, such as home offices or residential facilities in the workplace itself (the rectory, the White House, the embassy, the headmaster's house, the apartment above the store). (There is an important research task to be performed in simply documenting the extent of such coextensive home-workplaces and their effects on family behavior and relationships, as well as the dilemmas they create for those who are more peripheral to the work, such as wives and children—or husbands, as traditional roles change.)

Parker (1967) developed a conceptual scheme that can help differentiate between occupations with varying degrees of absorptiveness, by distinguishing between those where family is an extension of work, those where it is neutral and has minimal contact, and those where it is opposed, as in the following chart.

FIGURE I

Three Kinds of Relations between Work and Family Based on Degree of
Occupational Absorptiveness of Husband's Work*

Relationship between Arenas:	Work-Home Extension (positive relationship)	Minimal Contact (neutral relationship)	Work-Home Opposition and Competition (negative relationship)
Husband's Occupation	farming, small shop or business, some professional or craft work	technical, routine, bureaucratic, clerical, low- and mid-level managerial	mining, fishing, low-skill factory work
Occupational Characteristics	home and work locales at least partly co-extensive	low visibility of occupation to family	psychologically or physically exhausting, damaging work
Husband's Family Role in Relation to Occupational Role	continuous with work	alternative to work	recuperation from work
Wife's Role in Relation to Husband's Occupation	collaborative	supportive	peripheral

*Adapted from Parker, 1967: 49.

Employing organizations as well as occupations may themselves vary in their "greediness." (See Coser, 1974, for

27

discussion of the concept, though not in this context.) Some define roles for employees' families, trying to absorb them, while others do not enter this area at all. Some large businesses studied in the 1950s had stringent criteria for corporate wives, while others were much looser and appeared uninterested in the family lives of executives (Whyte, 1952). Even within the same occupational category, then, there can be considerable variation in the absorptive potential of work, depending on specific organizational arrangements. Here the social organization of work and its organizational environment determine the extent of involvement of the family. I have elsewhere (Kanter, 1977) defined five conditions that tend to activate an organization's demands on the wives of top role-players to participate actively in their husbands' jobs and careers: (1) *In small cities and towns.* If the organization plays a major role in the community in which it is located, if it is a major employer, it needs good community relations and counts on wives to help. There is also a tendency for organization leaders to be public figures in the town and wives to become known. Their lives may be shaped by community service in which they serve as organization diplomats. (2) *In political situations.* When the organization (or leaders) need to win continual approval from constituents, to win votes or to raise funds from donors or to secure favorable legislation, its diplomatic apparatus becomes important, and it consequently becomes more absorptive of wives. Wives of top politicians have major roles to play. Service organizations, such as hospitals, often create women's auxiliaries, with an expectation that members' wives will be active. (3) *In "total institutions."* If the organization constitutes more than a workday involvement and provides housing or other domestic services for members, as in the military or for staffs of boarding schools or small-town colleges, wives become involved for two reasons. The boundary between work and nonwork life becomes fuzzy with the organization encompassing much of members' lives; and the greater legitimacy needs of such demanding organizations makes it more important to secure the support of families. A survey of wives of headmasters of private schools, for example, showed how much more constraining the wife's role was, how much more she had to do, in boarding schools (the total institution situation) compared with day schools (Kanter, 1977: Chapter 5, note 27). (4) *In controversy.* Where the

28

organization is controversial or makes controversial decisions the diplomacy performed by unpaid volunteers, such as wives, is important. (5) *In entrepreneurial climates and times of change.* When the organization is growing, transforming itself, or facing a rapidly changing environment, it can make use of new connections made socially with other systems (part of wives' jobs as hostesses); it needs to count on the total dedication and achievement drives of top-ranking members (and therefore on the motivation, understanding, assistance, and support of spouses); and it can benefit from the ties of wives and family members to the community, a source of useful information. Wives of entrepreneurs often play critical roles in their husbands' businesses.

The role of wives rather than husbands is stressed here, because there seems to be no "corporate husband" equivalent thus far to the "corporate wife." There has also been a great deal more attention paid to the consequences for wives in such situations than to the consequences for children or other kin relations— issues that warrant investigation. It is additionally clear that the constraints imposed on the family of workers in highly absorptive occupations do not always allow wives (or others) to participate directly in the job. They may suffer feelings of exclusion from the work setting at the same time that their own lives are tightly constrained by what happens within it. Thus, the "career" of the "organization wife" (paralleling the husband's career stage) may be framed as a series of dilemmas: managing exclusion or inclusion when the job creates husband-absence; balancing instrumentality/sentimentality in the formation of social relationships, when the job constrains sociability; and handling publicness/privacy, when the job intrudes on private life (Kanter, 1977). Warner and Abegglen (1955, 1956) also identify several different role choices for corporate wives.

One illustration of the relevance of degree of occupational absorptiveness to the family-work connection is a study of clergy marriages (Scanzoni, 1965). While this is a field that tends to be high on absorptiveness to begin with, the kind of church in which the minister is employed makes a difference in the freedom of the wife and children. Two kinds of settings were identified: sect type (expecting separation from the world and total involvement) and church type (permitting more freedom of involvement with the surrounding world). In the sect type settings the wives were expected to perform many assistant pastor duties, and they were to serve as models of virtue—their habits, speech, dress, child-rearing, etc., were to be at a higher moral level, defined by religious standards, and above reproach. Similarly, husbands in the sect type settings tended to put church work above their families and remained "on call" even during leisure hours. (One consequence was the much more limited expressiveness and companionship in the sect type families.) Absorptive occupations thus create pressures and standards for family members other than the officially employed workers, and the efforts and performances of those others can enter into the functioning of the work system.

Absorptive occupations can be said to be modern versions of family productive systems, although often the family is dominated by an organization it does not control. As such, they are one of the most important places in which work-family connections need to be examined, for in these kinds of work, occupational systems constrain and implicate the whole family directly, immediately, and routinely, just as family dynamics may affect the work system. The benefits and costs of absorption of families into work settings could be examined by looking at intentional communities where work and personal life are highly —and voluntarily—integrated (Zablocki, 1971; Kanter, 1972a, 1973; French and French, 1975) as well as those in which families are absorbed against their interests. There is a need for more research to guide social theory and social policy here. For policy, especially, questions about the right of organizations to demand total absorption, the benefits and costs to families in these positions, and what organizations owe to the spouses and families of workers in absorptive pursuits may become significant social welfare questions of the future.

It is also important to distinguish between *qualitative* aspects of work absorption or overload (as in mental or emotional absorption) and *quantitative* aspects (as in temporal absorption where there is too much to do to confine it to work time). (French et al.'s research, 1965, on overload and stress for university professors versus administrators makes this useful distinction.) Quantitative absorption involves time as a scarce resource.

30

The amount of time demanded by occupations and the timing of occupational events are among the most obvious and important ways occupational life affects family life. Family events and routines are built around work rhythms (at least more generally than the reverse), just as much of the timing of events in the society as a whole (e.g., the opening and closing of stores, which television programs are shown at night) is predicated on assumptions about the hours, days, and months when people are most likely to be working or not working. The sheer number of hours spent at work as well as which part of the day those hours encompass can influence a large number of family processes through, for example, the effects of fatigue or the availability of the worker to take responsibility for or participate in family events. Whether work-related activities extend beyond the formal hours officially devoted to "work" and intrude upon time the family expects to claim can similarly affect the quality of family life. How the hours which workers have available for leisure and family synchronize with those of the other family members and the possibilities which society makes available for those hours is another issue. Finally, work which does not permit stable daily rhythms to develop or disrupts daily routines—such as work which involves a great deal of travel—also constrains the possibilities for family organization. Despite the importance of these issues, remarkably little research on them exists.

There has been considerable discussion and some controversy over how many hours Americans actually work. There seems to be general agreement that blue-collar workers in some industries work shorter official weeks than one hundred years ago; for example, the work week is below forty hours in printing and publishing and women's apparel manufacturing (Henle, 1962). However, the decline in the work week for the United States economy as a whole over the century may be offset somewhat by dual job holding, which increased from 3 percent in 1950 to 5.3 percent in 1957 (Zeisel, 1958; see also Carter, 1970). Swados (1958) also concluded that for factory workers less work might mean less leisure. He guessed that among Akron rubber workers with an official six-hour, six-day work week, perhaps 14 to 20 percent held a second full-time job and 40 percent a second part-time job. For the self-employed and professionals there is not much dispute that working hours are not decreasing. Higher occupational groups tend to work much longer hours than low-prestige occupations, and high income men work at least fifty hours a week (Wilensky, 1961). A 1957 *Fortune* survey showed that executives spent sixty or more hours per week working (Riesman, 1958). Even within professional ranks there are great differences in the number of working hours. In a Detroit survey of several occupations Wilensky (1961) found that a much larger proportion of lawyers and professors worked over forty-five hours a week, whereas about one-half of the engineers studied worked less than forty-five hours. The self-employed, from small proprietors to solo lawyers, worked over fifty-five hours per week. In a small Minneapolis study professors had a fifty-six to sixty hour work week, including evening and weekend work done at home; advertising men, a forty-five hour week, with work brought home only rarely; and dentists, a forty hour work week, with work never brought home (Gerstl, 1961). Carter (1970) argued that the shift in the occupational distribution toward services would also increase working hours for more people, since service occupations tend to take more time and to be better liked than factory jobs. It appears, then, that among the employed the only occupational category for which working hours have actually decreased may be white-collar occupations, such as clerical and low level administrative jobs. (Young and Willmott, 1973, suggest this in the British context.) Willmott (1971) also indicated that such white-collar staff brought little work home compared to executives and did little overtime compared to factory workers.

The variations in hours worked among occupational categories affect the possibilities for family arrangements. The lower middle class, the category with the shortest actual working hours, also has the most egalitarian "companionate" marriages—perhaps in part a function of the greater temporal availability of husbands to share chores and act as companions to their wives. One study showed that joint husband-wife leisure participation was highest in the lower middle class (Adams and Butler, 1967). The professors in another study worked the longest hours (compared to dentists and advertising men), brought home the most work, and in addition were thus the least likely to spend much time with their children and most likely to do *no* household chores (Gerstl, 1961). The spillover of work time into leisure time is also a problem for executives, who are most likely to bring home work problems despite the long hours in the office and whose irritability and lack of attention at home can generate work-family conflict (Willmott, 1971). Husbands' occupational attributes also act as structural constraints on their time and motivation to contribute to family activities and therefore significantly affect the opportunity structure of married women (Mortimer, Hall, and Hill, 1976).

Shift workers have other work-family issues due to their hours and the way they affect the expected synchrony between work and nonwork events (Aldous, 1969). One study discovered that each shift carried its own characteristic family problems. There was more friction between husband and wife for *night*-shift workers and more trouble with the father role for *afternoon*-shift workers (Mott et al., 1965). Levinson et al. (1962) found that shift work, in their study of a large midwestern company, produced added psychological burdens, in that workers could not establish regular eating and sleeping patterns. But for those preferring isolation, shift work relieved them of community and family responsibilities. Night workers have not been carefully researched, but journalistic accounts (Smith, 1974) and recent research (Lein et al., 1974) suggest some of the family issues they face. For one night manager of a grocery store, the major cost was the stress engendered by the limited time the family had to spend together and problems with his wife because of their limited social life, especially Saturday night when her friends were all going out. On the other hand, night workers may also be able to help with the housework, errands, and greeting the children when they come home from school, but when night work fosters a strong occupational community, as among craft printers (Lipset, Trow, and Coleman, 1956), the family may lose importance as a focus of primary ties. In any case, families have to organize their lives around the schedule of night workers. Such workers may total about 4 percent of the labor force in Massachusetts (Smith, 1974) and include a range of occupations from policemen to reservations clerks in airports.

The case of shift and night workers makes clear that it is not only the *amount* of time available for family and leisure that is an issue but its *timing*. Since other family members have their own priorities and schedules, and since society makes certain events possible only at certain times, timing becomes important in determining the effects of working hours. Lein and associates (1974) have documented the ways in which two-worker families work out their scheduling issues, as well as the effects of schedules on family relations. Husbands who are home during the day can more easily help with child care, even though wives who do the housework may feel they lose their "job autonomy." Fathers with pre-school children often preferred the night shift, hoping to change to a day shift when their children began to attend school.

One striking example of issues created by schedule problems is the failure of some experiments with a four-day week. In 1958 an aircraft parts plant in California provided workers with a three-day weekend a month without a reduction in the total hours worked; once a month they had a free Monday. Despite initial enthusiasm, workers voted to discontinue the system after less than a year. Some of the complaints make clear how much the *timing* of free time may have been at fault: e.g., the time was used for home chores that could as easily have been done on Saturdays, it was lonely at home on Mondays with everyone else at work or at school, and daytime television was designed for women and children (Meyersohn, 1963). In other words, a lump of free time out of synchrony with the rhythms of the rest of the family and the rest of society may not improve the quality of family life at all. As Riesman (1958) suggested after reporting a 1957 Roper poll indicating some negative feelings about the four-day week, housewives may not be eager to have their husbands underfoot on one of *their* working days.

A different kind of time experiment, however, also makes apparent the intertwining of work hours and family life but with more positive effects. Flexible working hours or *flextime* (a word coined by Willi Haller in Germany) is now in widespread operation throughout Europe and is gradually being introduced in some United States companies. Within specified limits employees choose their own hours. There is already evidence of its positive effects (Wade, 1973; Stein, Cohen, and Gadon, 1976). (Among other benefits, when enough organizations in a community institute flextime, it lessens traffic congestion and cuts down on commuting time. See Racki, 1975.) One example is a male bank supervisor who was able to adjust his schedule to leave work at 3 P.M. rather than 4:30, with profound effects on his relationships with his family.

Previously he had gotten home after fighting traffic in time to wash up, say hello to everyone, try to unwind, and then have dinner. By the time dinner was over, he would feel too tired to start any projects, particularly working on a boat, which was his hobby. Often he would have to drive his wife to go shopping or would just flop in front of the television set. When he was able to come home earlier, he found that there was enough time to begin working on the boat in the afternoons. His kids would be home from school feeling fairly fresh, and soon his two boys began to join him in working on the boat. While he was doing that, his daughter was able to take his wife shopping with the car which he had brought home, and when they returned, they would all eat. Since he had gotten a good start in the afternoon on the boat, he often would be in the mood to go back to it in the evening. So, as a consequence, his relationships with his sons became much closer. He enjoyed his wife more because they could do activities separately which interested them individually and still have more time together. And he was also picking up about a half hour in travel time each day, being able to come in early in the morning and go home when there was no traffic. (Cohen, 1975.)

European research on flextime suggests some other effects on personal life. In one survey in a Swiss company 35 percent of the workers (and men much more than women) used the flexible hours for spending more time with their families; married women tended to use them to provide more time for domestic chores (in keeping with the highly traditional sex role allocation in Switzerland). Almost 95 percent of all employees (the sample size was 1,500) were in favor of flextime—45 percent because of the way it improved the organization of private life. Married women with children were the most enthusiastic of all groups, not surprisingly (Racki, 1975). In another case, this time American, flextime also had dramatic effects on the work-family problem for a black mother employed in a Boston bank.

Though she was a good worker otherwise, her continual late arrival at work had upset her supervisor enough to consider firing her. It had also fed stereotypes about unreliability and laziness in the black community. When that particular office went on flexible working hours, to everyone's amazement the woman began to come in half an hour *earlier* than the previous starting time. It turned out that she'd been late because she had to drop her son in a day-care center and could just never quite get to the office by starting time. When she had the option of coming in earlier and being paid for it, she was able to make alternative arrangements and drop the child at a relative's house, which not only allowed her to get to work on time but relieved her anxiety considerably. This is a nice example of how flexible working hours facilitate the trade-off between private needs and work needs in a way that can allow choices to be made most effectively. (Cohen, 1975.)

For working women in traditional kinds of families, single parents with sole responsibility for children, or men who expect to share family tasks, flextime seems to permit a more comfortable synchrony of work and family responsibilities. Social policy as well as scientific knowledge would benefit from further research on this organizational change.

Work-related travel poses another time issue for families. If executive husbands and fathers have little time left over after their very long working days to be helpers to wives and companions to children, they are available *none* of the time when they travel. Renshaw (in press) studied 128 managers and wives in a large multinational corporation for which extensive travel was a job requirement. All felt burdened and stressed by the travel except two people: one single female manager and one man who used travel to escape from his family. The problems included: disconnected social relations, especially for the men; increasing responsibility for the wives, since virtually no areas of family life could be assigned to the husbands who were away so frequently; guilt on the part of the husbands for "deserting" their families; fatigue stemming from the travel itself; wives' fears of being alone; and extra worry for one another while the spouses were apart. Other scholars have mentioned additional travel-related problems: infidelity and a growing gap in the knowledge and life experiences of husbands and wives (Levinson, 1964; Seidenberg, 1973). If fathers are often absent, the family system may begin to close itself off to them, making re-entry difficult. Important events may occur without them, and the person who has been family leader in their absence may not want to give up the role. (One solution to the travel problem is to *increase* the work-family connection and find ways for traveling workers to bring their families along, short of those space-rooted functions that require a permanent involvement. In one unique situation, an executive of a medium-sized, commodity-producing company who commuted between cities made his wife an executive; and now they commute together along with their six-year-old child, who attends school part-time in one city and has a part-time tutor in the other.)

There are many other kinds of workers for whom travel or geographical movement or unusual schedules pose time difficulties, limiting the possibilities for certain kinds of family organization and even, in some cases, precluding the development of stable families at all. Traveling salesmen are one example among more prosperous workers. Seasonal and migrant laborers are an important example among the relatively downtrodden, who may find it difficult to establish those rhythms of private life that contribute to well-being (see Nelkin, 1970). On the other hand, seasonal schedules can also facilitate a working father's or mother's involvement with children, as in the case of teachers with long vacations or construction workers who have slack periods (Lein et al., 1974). All of these cases again make apparent the need to consider occupational rhythms as a critical factor in family life.

Daily, weekly, and yearly rhythms are not the only way work time and timing enter into family life. There is also a longer term aspect: the way the timing of major career events over the life cycle of the worker and major family events over its life cycle intersect and interact. Both Aldous (1969b) and Rapoport and Rapoport (1965) stress the importance of a developmental perspective in considering work-family interactions. Length of professional training and time of anticipated first earnings may affect a man's decision to marry (Rapoport, 1964). Marriage may affect a blue-collar worker's decision about remaining in the factory or taking the risks involved in changing jobs or getting more training (Chinoy, 1955). The fact that an organization man's biggest effort to gain promotions occurs at the same time in life that he has produced young children, necessitating that his wife take sole responsibility for them, may affect the kind of family system that is established (Aldous, 1969b) and generate later family problems. Steiner (1972) has written about the problems in executive families at the husband's "mid-life identity crisis." A man who has been alienated from his family during his climb to the top, leading his wife to seek her own satisfactions elsewhere, may suddenly turn to his family for support at the peak of his "success," only to find them no longer available. He describes the case of a man with psychosomatic complaints, whose children were in psychotherapy and whose wife was depressed and had sexual dysfunctions.

The timing and frequency of geographic relocations also have great impact on family life. Wives and children (along with husbands in some cases, now that professional women may be making their own decisions to make a move) may be uprooted at critical times in their own "careers," for example, just as they feel established and successful in their activities in a community. Several effects on wives of businessmen relocating frequently have been noted. Among them are wives' increased dependence on husbands and husbands' social contacts, decreasing their potential for an independent life; a greater number of pregnancies, with the wife carrying the baby with her to feel more secure in the new place and to serve as an excuse for not making immediate connections with the new community; and emotional stresses from depression to alcoholism (Renshaw, in press; Levinson, 1964; Weissman and Paykel, 1972; Seidenberg, 1973).

Changes in work situations (the occupation itself, employers, upward or downward mobility, relocation) have the effects they do on the family by virtue of the *family's* history and stage in its life cycle. A longer term, developmental perspective, such as this, has not been much in use in sociology and social psychology, although Wilensky (1961) has demonstrated the importance of work-life history as a variable in leisure and community participation. However, many of the critical influences and stresses generated by simultaneous work and family memberships have to do precisely with life history events.

The importance of time and timing, of course, also depends heavily on the *meaning* assigned to events. Studies of mothers employed in the paid labor force, for example, have indicated that it is the quality of parenting time, not the quantity, that makes a difference to the child. Similarly, to look at hours at home or away without considering what is done with those hours and what they mean to the people using them would be foolish indeed. Americans of different social positions put very different priorities on their use of time (see, e.g., White, 1955; Clarke, 1956; Wright and Hyman, 1958; there is also useful time budget research available). However, given this caveat, it is still important to look more closely at the ways in which work, as a time-consuming activity, influences and impacts upon the organization of family life. This should be investigated both across occupational categories and within them.

Another tradition considers the job largely as a source of reward: material and/or psychic. The rhythm and setting of work may affect its rewardingness, but these are not the variables considered important in linking work to family life; instead, the important variables have to do with the exchangeable resources (money or prestige) generated by the job. This line of reasoning lies behind the large number of studies of income or occupational prestige as correlates of life-style and family patterns. Most investigations that purport to study occupations and family life belong to this category. Many social class analyses of the state-and-rate form assign a rank or level to the husband-father's occupation and indicate what proportion of people or families in each group exhibit the predicted private behavior, attitude, event, or state. While the groupings tend to be called "classes," the assignment of prestige ranks as determinants of consumption style is actually closer to the Weberian definition of "status" than the Marxist notion of "class" as stemming from relationship to the means of production. Research in this area runs from fairly sophisticated and theoretically grounded to pedestrian and simpleminded. It remains compelling because of the large number of variables that show predictable patterning when gross occupational levels are differentiated, especially those variables having to do with the relative degrees of reward generated at each level. However, a great deal of variance within classes and similarity between classes still remains unexplained.

If income helps determine life-style and consumption level, it also determines very directly the relative resources over which each family member has initial control. Occupations are relevant to family life in this style of analysis only insofar as they generate "outputs" that have exchange value in the society. Money is the primary and most general one and the resource most frequently investigated, with prestige next (even though occupational status or prestige is often used as a surrogate for income). It is conceivable that occupations can sometimes provide other resources usable in the family, e.g., access to special rewards (such as introductions to famous people) or to special weapons (buddies on the police force).

In any case the relative possession of resources and economic contribution to the family can determine (a) the family's general level of tension or integration and (b) the relative power of family members. Economic security has been viewed as a "virtual prerequisite" for marital happiness (Furstenberg, 1974), as attested to by the large number of studies linking marital dissatisfaction to low income. The limited prospects for stable income and the greater earning potential of women have been used as explanations for divorce, desertion, and mother-headed families among poor blacks as well as the more limited authority of fathers in low income families: the value of their resources is not proportionately greater, if at all greater, than the resources of the wives. Working wives with an independent source of income may have more power than those who stay at home with no independent income (Aldous, 1969a; Gillespie, 1971). Finally, some studies of the effects of unemployment from the depression and later showed that men who became unemployed initially lost power in the family, especially if respect and authority were contingent on earnings (Cavan, 1959; Angell, 1936). After his studies of divorce, Goode commented that "willful failure in the role of breadwinner is often met by willful destruction of the sexual and social unity" of the marriage (1956: 63).

In a dynamic extension of the reward framework, Scanzoni (1970) developed and tested an exchange theory of the effects of location in the economic structure on family cohesiveness and expressiveness in the family. He argued that economic and psychic income from the job affects the presence or absence of marital tension. There is an overlap or linkage between economic and conjugal systems mediated by the male occupational role. The more a man is integrated into the economic opportunity structure (as measured objectively by his occupational status, education, and income and subjectively by his alienation or lack of alienation), the greater is the cohesiveness of the family and satisfaction with the husband-wife relationship, since the husband brings status and income into the family to exchange for services and positive feelings. However, especially on higher levels, income alone is not enough. Wives, he found, are more positively motivated to respond to their husbands the more the husband provides in the way of prestige and education. The greatest effects were in communication and understanding, which declined markedly when the husband did not "provide" according to the wife's expectations. On the other hand, "adequate provision" generated in exchange much satisfaction in this area. At the same time, deprivation of status rewards tended to generate feelings of hostility, especially for wives. More advantaged parents communicated positive achievement orientations to children, while less advantaged parents communicated greater caution and docility. Lack of integration with the economic opportunity structure and lack of ability to bring rewards into the family seemed to Scanzoni a prime cause of the displacement of economic discontents onto personal relations as well as an explanation for tensions between family members.

One criticism of the exchange model in the rewards and resources area is its almost exclusive focus on economic and political relations between family members. The underlying quality of family life portrayed in the model is one of constant contingency and bargaining. While this might indeed accurately represent *some* families, it also leaves out a range of family life variables, including cultural traditions, values, love and affection, and other issues of the family as a system that are not captured by a simple economic exchange framework. The ways that external rewards and resources feed into family life are not so simple and not so linked to contingent behaviors in a rational calculus (so much of this for so much of that). For example, it could be argued that the lack of external resources leads to the impoverishment of internal family life *not* because breadwinners thus lose authority and spouses and children refuse to do *their* part, but because it limits the quality of life for the family as a whole. Lack of external resources may restrict choice, narrow the possibility for overlapping interests between and among family members, provide fewer opportunities for leisure and self-expression, limit the possibilities for life-enriching cultural pursuits, limit the chances to purchase load-reducing, outside services, etc. These issues need to be investigated.

To refine understanding of the reward and resource mediated work-family links requires more than a look at family dynamics at various reward levels. (We already know a great deal about this.) It also requires understanding of all the possible rewards and costs carried by jobs and the meaning and relative salience of these for family members.

41

A fourth aspect of work-family linkage concerns the cultural
dimensions of jobs. Occupations not only generate their own
cultures and thus views of appropriate life-styles, they also
generate a characteristic outlook on the world because of the
conditions in which they occur. Similarly, organizational
membership and the characteristics of positions within
organizations may also generate distinctive cultures and outlooks.
Marxist analysis offers one version of this argument: material
conditions, principally the person's relationship to the means of
production, shape consciousness. It is not necessary to assume
that jobs make deep inroads on the personality to assert that they
generate an outlook on the world and an orientation to self and
others. Occupations are important socializers and teachers of
values, especially those like the professions that come to
constitute "communities" with shared normative standards for
conduct, even outside of work. Hughes has been one of the
outstanding scholarly influences in this area, pointing out the
ways in which occupational groups build up "collective
representations." He argued that people's work provides a
subculture and an identity that become part of their personalities;
the culture, technique, etiquette, and skill of the profession
appear as "personality traits" in the individual (Hughes, 1958).

Within this area scholars have paid perhaps the most attention
to the effects of work situations on child-rearing values and
standards. Here it is assumed that parents take their cues for
desirable behavior and styles of interaction from what they see
as necessary for success in their own work milieux and that they
(even unconsciously) translate learned-on-the-job modes of
relating to their children. There are two major studies (for which
data were collected only a few years apart in the 1950s), which
dichotomized the occupational world as a whole in very
different ways. Kohn (1959, 1963, 1968), using traditional class
analysis, focused on how the blue-collar/white-collar distinction
in working conditions generated very different sets of parental
values. Miller and Swanson (1958) argued, on the other hand,
that class distinctions were less important than the critical
difference in outlook of those in entrepreneurial situations
compared with those employed in welfare bureaucracies.

Kohn's research is the more traditional and, in many ways, the less controversial of the two studies. He first differentiated the nature of white-collar and blue-collar work as it might affect world view. White-collar work involved manipulating ideas, symbols, and interpersonal relations; blue-collar work involved manipulating physical objects, with less skill required. White-collar work is usually more complex, requiring greater flexibility, thought, and judgment, with less supervision, while blue-collar work may be more standardized and more supervised. Kohn then predicted that these differences would be associated with child-rearing values and practices. He found blue-collar parents valued obedience, while white-collar parents tended to care most about internalized standards of conduct and value self-direction and initiative in children (Kohn, 1959, 1963, 1968; Kohn and Carroll, 1960). The two sets of parents also defined parental roles differently, varying in whether mothers thought it most important that fathers should be supportive (white-collar) or directive (blue-collar) and whether fathers agree with mothers (white-collar) or refuse to get involved at all (blue-collar). (See Kohn and Carroll, 1960.) Many of Kohn's findings have been replicated (Pearlin, 1970; Gecas and Nye, 1974).

Inkeles (1955, 1960) had also found earlier that across eleven countries middle-class parents more often stressed ambition, while working-class parents emphasized obedience to authority. However, some class-based differences in socialization based on this reasoning also seem to be collapsing over the last decades (Brofenbrenner, 1971), and the difference in values between *fathers* in the two categories is much greater than the difference between *mothers* (Gecas and Nye, 1974). McKinley (1964) also found the differences over three classes between fathers greater than between mothers, with mothers in general tending toward the more "middle-class" use of reasoning and verbal sanctions. (One can argue that the working conditions for mothers and housewives—their material conditions and "class" position as individuals—are more similar over a variety of income levels and husbands' occupations than the working conditions for men. I will return to this point later.) There seems to be some merit to the proposition, then, that what people see at work, as defined by a manual/nonmanual distinction, helps shape the family's outlook toward the proper behavior of and toward children.

Miller and Swanson divided the occupational world differently.

The most important feature of the modern work world, they argued, was the growth of a new condition of employment in the welfare bureaucracy, and this relatively recent development was creating a new world view that parents were transmitting to their children. The new bureaucratic outlook contrasted with the more traditional mass-entrepreneurial ethic of independent achievement and individual responsibility. This distinction of outlook would cut across and transcend class levels as well as account for differences in orientation within classes. Miller and Swanson defined as entrepreneurial conditions independent and isolated work and birth outside of United States cities. Entrepreneurial fathers tended to work in organizations of small size, simple division of labor, relatively small capitalization, and with provision for mobility and income through risk-taking and competition. Bureaucratic fathers, on the other hand, were urban native-born, along with their wives, worked for someone else in organizations with three or more supervisory levels, and derived their income primarily through wages or salaries, so that their working conditions involved both more security and more emphasis on the ability to develop smooth relations within the organization. This distinction was one of "integration setting" rather than class or occupational category, since there was no significant difference in the random sample in the proportion of each condition in four social classes or in the husband-father's occupation, although the bureaucratic parents tended to have more education.

Accordingly, Miller and Swanson argued that entrepreneurial mothers would be more likely to emphasize a child's development of strong self-control and an independent and actively manipulative approach to the world. Bureaucratic mothers would be less interested in self-control than accommodation, would permit more impulse expression, and would teach children to seek direction from others. The predictions were confirmed by and large, although there were a few interesting class differences that could also be accounted for by working conditions. (E.g., among the upper middle-class, bureaucratic parents, a slightly more "entrepreneurial" outlook on self-control tended to prevail. At these levels even bureaucrats need achievement and risk-taking skills.) Class comparisons for each integration setting yielded no significant differences, indicating, for example, that bureaucratic parents were much more alike than different, even if their class position was different. The Miller and Swanson analysis tended to confirm the importance of the structure of the work *context,* as opposed to occupational *status,* in shaping world views, which in turn shape important aspects of family life.

There are some problems in both the Kohn and Miller and Swanson studies. Miller and Swanson, even more than Kohn, make an almost magical leap from condition of *father's* employment to *mother's* world view. The actual role of the husband-father in the family and how his occupational circumstances are transmitted to the wife are never made clear in the Miller and Swanson case, although Kohn does treat the first issue. The Aberle and Naegele (1952) interviews make clear that middle-class fathers, at least, have strong feelings on these matters around sons. A spin-off investigation, using the Miller and Swanson categories and data, does suggest some ways in which integration setting affects marital power structure and task allocation, thus presumably also having impact on the wives (Gold and Slater, 1958). In the mass-entrepreneurial context, for example, family welfare and status depend almost entirely on the competitive achievements of the husband or on the wife's efforts alongside his in a small family business. In such cases, orientations easily transfer to the wife-mother. However, the results of this study were far from clear-cut. The connections between work-determined world view and child-rearing orientations still need much more explanation, with the intervening links and the behavior of *all* family members included.

These studies also use global indicators of work conditions and leave a great deal of the variance unexplained. Attempts to differentiate occupational cultures *within* the manual/nonmanual and entrepreneurial/bureaucratic categories or to develop other cross-cutting dimensions might succeed in explaining more of the variance, especially in studies of social class. There are a few exploratory efforts to make the translation of outlooks from an occupational milieu, differentiated into several specific types, into family life. Steinmetz (1974) did a small-scale pilot study on the use of actual and threatened physical punishment on adolescents as a function of occupation, since this behavior was found *not* to be related to social class. Physical punishment frequency was highest among fathers in "persuasive" occupations, such as business executives and salesmen who identify with power and strength and seek control in relationships. Next highest were "motoric" occupations, such as dentists and truck drivers, assumed to prefer concrete methods of problem-solving, using physical skills but not too dominating. At the bottom with least frequent instances of "violence" were supportive occupations (teachers, social workers) and conforming ones (accountants, clerks).

Gerstl (1961) pointed out that occupational milieux shape "tastes" as well as what are considered relevant and worthwhile leisure pursuits. Although there is a rather large literature on social class differences in leisure (e.g., White, 1955; Clarke, 1956; Swados, 1958; Wilensky, 1961; Meyersohn, 1963), Gerstl is one of the few scholars to relate leisure to occupational culture. Independent professionals (represented by dentists), organization men (advertising men), and salaried intellectuals (college professors) varied in their hobbies, likelihood of taking work home, whether the family home was a priority for leisure (advertising men more than dentists more than professors), time spent with children, and likelihood of doing household chores (dentists most of both, professors least). The occupational culture also influenced family culture. The advertising men were highly convivial, with frequent cocktail parties a part of their life. The professors engaged in the most intellectual and "cultural" pursuits and were negative about television. Here it becomes very clear that occupations affect families through distinctive world views. Rapoport and Rapoport (1965) provide other examples of the diffusion of occupational norms to the family: the story of Frank and Lillian Gilbreth (reported in their book, *Cheaper by the Dozen*), the time-and-motion industrial consultants who organized their home on the same efficiency basis.

The selection factor needs to be tested—whether people select jobs that reflect preexisting or latent world views. Roe (1956) has argued that personalities differ greatly from occupation to occupation, but it is not always clear, even in her studies, how much of the style was learned in the job itself. Indeed, it is striking just how little attention has been paid to work in studies of adult socialization. While there has been research on how people are socialized *into* jobs, there has been virtually none on the socialization effects of jobs for other life settings. Yet, not only do work situations carry characteristic orientations, they may also include specific and formal learning events that can

46

themselves have spillover potential. Some of these events relate directly to interpersonal styles, as does sensitivity training in industry. Wives have reported that after such experiences their husbands may come home with very different views of themselves, demands, and expectations of other family members; this sometimes introduces stress or requires readjustment (Kanter, 1977). The expanding or changing world view and learning potential of professional and managerial jobs has, of course, been offered as one explanation for the growing psychological gap between husbands and wives who stay at home (Levinson, 1964; Seidenberg, 1973). What jobs teach people and how they translate the learning into their primary relationships is an important topic for more careful and rigorous investigation.

Emotional Climate

Occupations contain an emotional climate as well that can be transferred to family life. That is, a person's work and relative placement in an organization can arouse a set of feelings that are brought home and affect the tenor and dynamics of family life. For some social scientists this kind of issue is the only major way that work and family systems are *directly* linked. McKinley (1964) argued that the geographical and social structural separation of work situations from family life made reasonable the use of psychological responses to work as an intervening variable between the organization of occupational and family worlds. In this line of thought, the influence of jobs stems from the psychological relation of persons to jobs and the emotional issues jobs might create for them that they take elsewhere to act out or resolve. Blauner, for example, proposed that peoples' relations to their work affect their entire personal and social being. He contrasted the craft printer's strong occupational ties, community involvement, self-esteem, and confidence with the more depressed and uninvolved state of textile workers (Blauner, 1964: 79-80).

Work satisfaction is one relevant variable. Some studies demonstrate that unpleasant, dissatisfaction-producing jobs are related to family tension. Hammond (1954), in an Australian study, found a direct and high correlation between the husband's work dissatisfaction and tension between family members. Bradburn and Caplovitz's (1964) studies of happiness found

47

some overall association between job tension and marriage tension. The husband's job satisfaction affected the whole tenor of family life for blue-collar families in a college town (Dyer, 1964). Presumably, happier families result when people feel good about themselves in connection with what they do at work and when they have fewer "gripes" to bring home. There is a fine ethnographic literature on the ways in which industrial work experiences "de-humanize" and decrease the possibilities for dignity and respect in the family (e.g., Sennett and Cobb, 1973; Aronowitz, 1973).

Tensions stemming from work environments have also been assumed to affect the hostility level in the family, particularly between parents and children. McKinley (1964) reasoned that deprivation, especially of approval, leads to frustration, which in turn leads to aggression in the form of hostility to others or regression and withdrawal. He proposed that the variations in prestige and social approval accorded to various occupations, as clustered in social classes, would correlate with the degree to which parents (especially fathers) were hostile and severe versus emotionally supportive to sons. Degree of autonomy in the work situation would also affect its emotional climate and hence whether the frustration-aggression hypothesis would hold. Those with less autonomy are more deprived of reward, more subject to control by others or external control (which leads to externalization of aggression), and not able to take out their frustrations on subordinates (so they must take them home). Therefore, a relationship between autonomy at work and hostility at home was also hypothesized.

McKinley's data are suggestive, though not unequivocal. (There are several methodological problems with his study. For one thing, he assumed the nature of the intervening links—declining approval and increasing emotional deprivation down the class ladder—but did not measure them directly, so that his correlations are between gross indicators of class and family variables. Autonomy, similarly, was not measured directly, except through a few questions to sons about supervision in their fathers' jobs, and was coded primarily by gross occupational category rather than direct inquiry. These problems are not uncharacteristic of research in this area.) Generally, through his own questionnaire and reanalysis of data from the Sears, Maccoby, and Levin studies of child-rearing, McKinley found that parents at lower levels of the class structure were more severe and hostile socializers than those at upper levels, with the percentage of people in this category increasing down the class ladder. Looking at the son alone, he found fathers to be less involved with their sons and not available as emotional supports at lower versus upper levels. Similarly, low autonomy tended to be associated with higher proportions of hostile and severe parents, especially fathers, although differences in autonomy had the most striking, clear-cut, and statistically significant effects in the predicted direction at the upper levels (what McKinley called the *upper class*—actually a combination of Hollingshead's Classes I and II). On the other hand, fathers were more likely to be less severe as socializers and more emotionally supportive and involved in sons' lives if their work had more power, satisfaction, and autonomy. Other studies also found that higher-class fathers were more supportive, accepting, and close (Kohn and Carroll, 1960) and that sons identified more with them (Williams et al., 1972).

The McKinley findings actually suggest that work autonomy or a similar emotional climate variable, such as control over work opportunities, may be more important than the gross measure of class, even though McKinley places his analysis in class terms. It is not surprising that relative autonomy showed the largest effects at the upper level, where absolute autonomy may be highest. At lower levels, where absolute autonomy may be low, relative degrees of it may make little difference.

Thus, McKinley's research can be taken as one indication of the possible effects of the emotional climate of occupations—how they make people feel—on relations in the family. This is the theme of Sennett and Cobb's (1972) studies of working-class men and their families. For example,

> The real impact of class is that a man can play out *both* sides of the power situation in his own life, become alternately judge and judged, alternately individual and member of the mass. This represents the "internalizing" of class conflict, the process by which struggle between men leads to struggle within each man. (Sennett and Cobb, 1972: 98.)

The notion that paternal authority over children can provide a substitute measure of "success" for men who feel defeated in the workplace is echoed by Blau and Duncan (1967: 428) in their examination of the American occupational structure. Steinmetz's (1974) exploratory study of occupational environments and use of physical punishment with children also points to the importance of style of control at work as a variable entering family life, even though her findings do not necessarily support those of McKinley. Fathers high on supervisory experience had high scores on an actual or threatened physical punishment index if they also appeared to value obedience, indicating that they felt they had the right to assert control.

Types of pressures and emotional demands are other aspects of emotional climate that can affect family life. Gerstl (1961) found in his study of seventy-five men in their forties predictable variation in the preferences for leisure "release" among members of three different occupations. Dentists, for example, tended to choose easygoing hobbies that allowed them to take things easy, while advertising men were inclined to want to "blow off steam" from their high pressure, competitive work. It is not uncommon for people in high interaction occupations to develop "interaction fatigue" and withdraw from contact at home. Wives of men in a corporate personnel training function, whose work involved deep involvement with others and sensitivity to subtle aspects of communication, reported in personal interviews that their husbands were often distant and insensitive when they came home, as though they had been "burned out" at work (Kanter, 1977). Finally, jobs are also sources of competing emotional attachment, both generally in the compellingness of some situations and specifically in the potential for infidelity.

Knowledge of the connections between the emotional climate of occupations and family dynamics is in a rudimentary stage. The relevant organizational dimensions which affect a person's experience still need to be identified. But three aspects of location in a work setting which have implications for out-of-work life can be suggested on the basis of field research and review of the organizational literature: relative *opportunity, power,* and *proportions* (Kanter, 1976b, 1977). Position in a structure of opportunity (chance to grow or move ahead) tends to define the degree of engagement or disengagement with a job and the height of a worker's aspirations, as well as affecting self-esteem. Relative power, in the sense of autonomy and ability to mobilize resources, tends to affect an individual's degree of flexibility or rigidity. The relatively powerless tend to seek control through rules-mindedness and domination of narrow territories. Finally, proportions (numerical representations of types of people—whether one is similar to or different from work peers) tends to shape a person's feelings of acceptance or stress in a work group and external support. (The effects of low opportunity, powerless, and isolated or "token" status on mental health and family relations are about to be tested in several organizational studies.)

The nature of the links between work experience and family life also need to be explored. Many important questions remain. Does the family world serve *compensatory* functions for emotional deprivations at work, or *displacement-of-aggression* functions (as McKinley's 1964 research suggests)? Does it get the best parts of a person's energy or commitment, when they are not called for at work, as Dubin's (1958) work hints, or does it get only the parts left over from an emotionally draining job? Do people orient themselves to the family emotionally in the same way they come to approach their work? The overwhelming tendency in social theory has been to assume the negative consequences for personal life of the experiences of alienation at work. Seeman (1967) has recently challenged this perspective, presenting Swedish data indicating that work alienation has few of the unpleasant personal consequences imagined. Yet other evidence does make a case for the spillover from the emotional connection with work to other areas of life. People with boring work tend to have boring leisure, and people with involving work have higher levels of both leisure and family involvement, even though the latter may work longer hours and bring home more work than the former (Willmott, 1971). Blue-collar workers in similar occupations at the same pay level tend to be more democratic in their politics and more creative in their leisure when their jobs permit more control, participation, and self-direction (Torbert and Rodgers, 1973).

This last study indicates along with others that knowledge of workers' formal occupational categories does not provide sufficient information on how their specific jobs might affect them and their families; instead, information on organizational and climate characteristics is needed. Gross categories, such as social class or even census job classification, are insufficient to elucidate the more subtle but real relationships between the organization of work and family life.

"The Family Fights Back":
Family Influences on Working
and the Work World

Most analyses of work and family in the modern American
context have settled into a comfortable economic determinism—
the centrality of work in setting the conditions for family life. No
equally compelling and tested framework exists for reversing the
relationship and looking at the effects of family patterns on work
systems in American society. There are several ways, however,
in which a reverse relationship may be suggested. All are subject
to further investigation.

First, cultural traditions carried by the family may be strong
enough to shape family members' decisions about their relation
to work and to enable them to resist pressures generated by
workplaces. Among certain ethnic groups, family life may be not
only carried out rather independently of workplace influences, but
family membership may seriously affect members' behavior as
workers. This has been argued for a number of immigrant groups,
especially Italian-Americans (Gans, 1962; McLaughlin, 1971)
and Irish (Dubnoff, 1975). Hareven, in historical studies of
French-Canadian textile workers, considered the family an
autonomous sphere, influencing individual work decisions, such
as who worked, when, where, and from what age, thus controlling

to some extent the labor supply of the employing organization. She wrote:

> Workers and immigrants [are] active agents, who despite the presence of powerful economic institutions exercised controls over the forces that tended to regiment them. . . . Newcomers to industrial society tended to shape the system to their own needs and subtly exercised a collective strength in their adaptation to industrial conditions, modifying the system to fit their wants and traditions. (1975b: 250.)

Reverse effects can be strong enough for some analysts to conclude that ethnicity is stronger than class in the United States as a determinant of life-style; Hareven argued that "working class" behaviors are an adaptation of ethnic patterns (1956:265).

Indeed, many early studies of class differences may have been picking up ethnic differences; working class "traditionalism" may have been in part a function of recency of arrival in America and closer connection with the old world culture. More current studies which find the development of a "new" or "modern" working class (with many behavioral similarities to the middle class) may be picking up, in part, the effects of generational assimilation (Handel and Rainwater, 1964; Rainwater and Handel, 1964). For this reason, Miller (1964a, b) locates the "stable working class" among the native-born alone. Yet, one must be cautious in interpreting this material as proving the cultural independence of the family in the face of occupational and economic constraints on life-style. Gans (1962) proposed that the very culture immigrants bring with them that shapes their response to American institutions in itself reflects the people's economic location in the old world. He contrasted the peasant origins of Italian immigrants with the more commercial life of old world Jews.

A second way in which the influence can run from personal relations to work systems lies in those areas of economic and occupational life in which family connections still define work relations. This is most likely to be true of the American aristocracy and of entrepreneurs operating within family firms. The upper-upper class has not been studied in social class analyses as much as the classes below, because of its relative rarity and ability to secure privacy from the public and researchers, although there are a few interesting descriptive accounts (Baltzell, 1958; Cavan, 1969) and analyses of the maintenance of class privilege through an insulated life-style (Mills, 1956). Zeitlin (1974) suggested that knowledge of the operation of American capitalism, including the large-scale corporate variety, requires investigation of family systems. As with ethnic groups, a strong case can also be made that the behavior of upper-class families reflects their economic position: that their lives may revolve around the preservation and transmission of material, institutional, and symbolic property (see Cavan, 1969; Farber, 1971); much of their behavior thus resembles that occurring in more traditional societies in which the family *is* the basic economic unit. But the fact that there is an economic explanation for the thrust of their life-style does not do away with the need, especially with these influential families, to study the family's behavior, relationships, and decisions as a shaper of economic and work life.

Family-based businesses, ranging from "mom and pop" stores to industrial firms largely owned by a single family for generations, represent another way in which the nature of family life can influence the structure of work life. Family ownership and control is still significant even in the largest corporations; one study estimated (conservatively) that over 42 percent of the largest *publicly* held corporations are controlled by one person or a family with a great deal of direct managerial involvement (Barnes and Hershon, 1976; see also Zeitlin, 1974). In such situations in which work and family are highly integrated, the effect of family system variables cannot be ignored. They also represent ideal situations in which to test a variety of assumptions (some described on pp. 8-17 and pp. 71-73) about the inherent tensions between family and work organization. Sociologists have generally ignored this challenge, although there is a fine study of Indian family firms' organization and decision making (Cohen, 1974). Barnes and Hershon (1976) showed that such firms' characteristic histories, as well as characteristic difficulties, could only be understood by careful analysis of the family systems. Family transitions (the passage of control from one generation to another) often occur simultaneously with organizational transitions, and, in general, family conflicts have a major impact on the organization. (See "Profitable Oedipus," 1975, for an interesting illustrative case.) The entrepreneur's wife has an important role to play, for example, in bridging the gap between fathers and sons. "Families are in business to stay," Barnes and

Hershon (1976) conclude, and thus their relations must be understood as an important part of organizational analysis.

Ethnic groups, upper-class families, and family firms all represent ways in which the family may exert a strong influence on work—or at least push back. There is also a weaker way: those situations in which family members get involved or implicated in the work of the worker. In the classic male breadwinner-housewife family, if the man is said to bring his relation to the workplace to the family, the woman can bring the family to the work organization. Where work is not confined to an hourly job in a separated workplace, performance of the "wife" role (in quotations because it could theoretically be played by husbands of employed wives) may be an almost mandatory part of the job, may influence the husband's career opportunities, and may even influence relationships within the work organization itself. The "corporate wife," as popularized by Whyte (1951, 1952) in his "organization man" studies, is a well-known but not well-investigated phenomenon. Corporate wives have been examined mostly from the point of how the husband's work puts intolerable pressure on the wife (Seidenberg, 1973), and not so much from the other perspective: how the wife's (or family's) activities may affect the performance at work and work opportunities, although Papanek (1973) moves close to this in her discussion of the "two-person single career." (See pp. 28-30 and Kanter, 1977, for a fuller discussion.)

Farm families, of course, can also act as a work unit, affecting work decisions, in part because the farm remains a family workplace. Straus (1958) compared the wives of farm settlers in a new project who showed high and low success. He found that the wives' background characteristics and material contributions (their own production) did not distinguish between the two groups. However, the wives' personal characteristics in relation to their husbands and the system did; wives of high-success men were more accepting of male dominance, more persevering, social, and responsible. Some agricultural experts have tied the future of the family farm to a new kind of marriage partnership, however, in which the wife is active in all aspects of farm management (Lublin, 1975).

Finally, if the emotional climate at work can affect families, so can a family's emotional climate and demands affect members as workers. Family situations can define work orientations, motivations, abilities, emotional energy, and the demands people bring to the workplace. In Goode's (1960) theory of role strain, the family acts as a "role budget center"; individuals must account to families for what they spend in time, energy, and money outside the family. For children, family background has been shown to affect school performance, achievement motivation, occupational choice, personal well-being, and general life changes (e.g., Lipset and Bendix, 1959; Turner, 1962; Rapoport, 1975a; Bowles and Gintis, 1976). For adults, the feelings of other family members toward the job may be communicated directly to occupants and affect their attitudes toward it (e.g., Dyer, 1956). Family status, the influence of family members, and changes, such as the introduction of a child, can affect career decisions (which in turn can have a cumulative effect on organizations): the willingness to take risks, the willingness or ability to travel.

Not surprisingly, many of these subjects have been studied or noted for employed *women* with families but not for men. Yet even though some men might have special reason to deny them, there is no reason to suppose that there might not be equally strong effects of family life on their work life. On September 4, 1975, for example, a widely shared family issue closed several plants in Louisville, Kentucky. Up to 60 percent of the blue-collar workers in some industries stayed home to protest court-ordered busing (*The Wall Street Journal,* September 5, 1975). A study in progress on divorced fathers indicates that men, even in demanding professional jobs, will restructure their work situation to accommodate part-time child care, making sure that they can leave early on certain days or even changing a full-time job (head of hospital unit) to part-time (Finkelstein and Rosenthal, in progress). Some men have even brought their children to the office when they cannot get babysitters, just as one powerful woman executive does. The men also began to question work achievement as the ultimate value in life.

Bailyn and Schein's research on men's careers has begun to make clear the extent to which men's work decisions are affected by their attachment to their families. The key to understanding careers, they argued in a number of papers, lies not in the person, the organization, or the work task itself, but rather in the ways in which cultural, organizational, and occupational demands interact with individual aspirations, work demands, and family concerns across time. In a sample of over 1,300 MIT alumni, they uncovered several different forms of work attachment, including the "accommodative" pattern, in which the demands of work are subordinated to those of family. In helping professions, this pattern may be associated with effective professional functioning because of value consistency, but in technical careers the accommodators tend to be more passive in their professional role, less likely to be active in professional affairs, to be entrepreneurs, to see themselves as good leaders, to be power-oriented or to be greatly concerned with the intrinsic character of work (Bailyn, 1976; see also Bailyn and Schein, 1976).

It is important to investigate for men as well as women, then, how family situations, emotional climates, culture and traditions, resources, and economic possibilities affect work situations, successes, and orientations.

Women's Work and Family Relations

Most of the material reviewed thus far was really about men's work, and most of it assumed that the man is the primary—or more likely the sole—breadwinner in the family. Some phenomena may be generalizable to women too: for example, the effects of occupational outlooks or emotional climate. However, women also have a variety of work roles assigned primarily to them, as a function of occupational segregation, and have traditionally at least (although changing rapidly) had an expected set of family responsibilities. Furthermore, the fact that women are also "workers" in families—whether paid or not—throws into question some routine assumptions about work and family and adds complicating variables when women are paid workers in the labor market outside the home. Thus, it is necessary to give separate attention to women and employment. The literature on determinants and correlates of women's labor force participation has been carefully and insightfully reviewed by Kahne (1975); here I turn to less economic and more social questions.

Even for sympathizers and supporters, research on women's work and family relations had generally been dominated by the traditional view of woman's place until the late 1960s. First, there was a "social problem" orientation toward women in the paid labor force, resulting in study of only those aspects of women's work that appear to create "problems." Since the jobs of housewife or community volunteer were assumed to fit the traditional conception of women's appropriate roles around which the institution of family is organized, the effects of these kinds of activities on personal relations and vice versa was little noted, with only a few exceptions (e.g., Caplow, 1954; Lopata, 1971). On the other hand, jobs in the paid labor force outside the home were assumed to generate role conflict or induce strain that must be managed—for women, although not usually for working men. This social problem approach to women's work entered the social science literature as early as 1909, when an article in the *American Journal of Sociology* asked "how women's access to industrial occupations reacted on the family" (Weatherly, 1909). Given this orientation, most studies consequently tried to see whether there were detrimental consequences to the children or the marriage as a result of mothers working. (The evidence is mixed, but there seems to be none, at least as the question is globally and simply stated. There are a few possible negative effects on sons and on blue-collar marriages. See Hoffman and Nye, 1974).

Another clue to the traditional assumptions underlying research in this area was the lack of attention paid to what the woman does when she works. The characteristics of a woman's work (income, prestige and status, hours and demands, or occupational culture) were virtually ignored before the new wave of research. The *fact* of employment itself was considered enough to affect other aspects of life. Only a few researchers had added one important qualifying variable: a woman's *connection* to or *feelings* about her work (Hoffman, 1961; Orden and Bradburn, 1969; Safilios-Rothschild, 1970; Bailyn, 1970). The assumption behind this absence of attention must have been that family is always the only salient realm for women. Even those women with high commitment to work (Safilios-Rothschild, 1970) were seen by researchers as interested in being employed but not necessarily in what they did. As one reads the literature, women would seem rather unconnected to their work and unaffected by it. (Certainly this view had been taken by employers for many years, to the detriment of women.)

This position is particularly important as ideology because it is the opposite of the assumption made for men—inaccurately, as it turns out—that work *is* their central life interest and the central organizing principle in their behavior and relations. Dubin (1956) tried to disprove this in his studies of industrial workers. Thus, researchers now are careful to differentiate the male labor force into those for whom work is not very salient (e.g., blue-collar workers) and those for whom it is highly salient (e.g., professionals). Ironically, one widely cited study confirming the high salience of work for professionals used a *female* professional group, nurses (Orzack, 1959).

The sexual asymmetry is very apparent. It is the *unemployed man* who was seen as a social problem, likely to have disturbed marital relations and likely to produce delinquent children. For women, it was the *employed woman* who was seen in *virtually the same ways.* Liberal researchers have come along to debunk or modify both stereotypes, particularly to disentangle the effects of poverty or race on earlier investigations of the negative aspects of working mothers. Yet in defining research around these conceptions, a large number of important questions were ignored. While the focus on the employed woman as the social problem has dominated until recently, a growing body of evidence suggests that *unemployment* for women may be the bigger problem. Working women are healthier, showing more self-acceptance, satisfaction with life, greater freedom from emotional disturbance, and fewer physical symptoms (Feld, 1963). A study of longevity, looking at who beat their life expectancy as calculated by actuarial tables and by how much, put housewives far down on the list, well behind blue-collar workers (Palmore and Stone, 1973). Intensive studies of depressed women showed that women who worked outside the home while depressed were less impaired in their functioning than housewives, and that this was *not a* function of differences in the severity of the illnesses, leading the researchers to conclude that there was "something protective in the work situation" (Weissman and Paykel, 1974: 72). Adolescent daughters of working mothers have higher achievement patterns, and elementary school children of full-time working black mothers have better social adjustments. Among the highly educated, the fact of a woman's work may increase marital satisfaction (Hoffman and Nye, 1974). In small families, employed mothers may get more pleasure from their children (Nye and Hoffman, 1963). On the other hand, the *unemployed* women in Holmstrom's (1972) study tended to be overly possessive mothers. In short, paid work seems good for women and their families.

Type of Work Determines Its Family Impact

It would also seem important to differentiate work setting, occupational milieux, and work-life histories for women in the same ways that they can be differentiated for men in order to examine more fully the work-family connections for women. We must assume that work characteristics—and not just the fact of employment alone—play an important role. For example, it is not surprising to note that in one of the few studies using women's work enjoyment as a variable, the higher status jobs were better liked and had more positive impact on the family (Hoffman, 1961). They are also the jobs, not coincidentally, that provide more responsibility, security, and autonomy and boost self-esteem. Whether a woman has an opportunity for self-expression and the exercise of power at work can be important, both for her own mental health and as a shaper of relationship orientations. We need to examine women's jobs as socializers as well as those of men. How the blocking or expression of women's aspirations at work (Kanter, 1977: Chapter 6) affects her family relations is important. In addition, many typical women's jobs may parallel a kind of family relationship—e.g., secretaries as office wives (Kanter, 1975; 1977: Chapter 4) teachers as mothers (Lightfoot, 1975)—the existence and effects of which should be studied. Do women with more traditional "female" jobs play more traditional roles at home? Similarly, the effects of bureaucratic versus entrepreneurial settings (Miller and Swanson, 1958) should be studied for women as well as men.

The consequences of the type of work-life history a woman has also deserve investigation. Wilensky's (1961) distinction between orderly and disorderly careers can be a useful explanatory variable for women as well as men. How the relative continuity or interruption of work or the extent to which work experiences constitute an orderly career relates to behavior in other realms is important. For example, in a small sample of families (Holmstrom, 1972), women with professional training but with disrupted work histories were much more likely to have traditional husband-dominant marriages than professional women who had worked uninterruptedly. Were these women also more conservative and conventional in other respects? Such questions deserve study.

Bringing the Husband Back In

A third problem with traditional research on women's work-family relations was an implication that a woman creates her marriage and raises her children alone. This is certainly true for the rising number of female-headed households, a group that deserves serious attention; but for married working mothers, it represents a major distortion. Where are the husband-fathers and their responsibilities in the family? Bailyn's (1970) attempt to study the joint effects of both husbands' and wives' relations to their work and a few small sample case accounts of two-career families (Rapoport and Rapoport, 1971; Holmstrom, 1972) and two-worker families (Lein, 1974) were the few exceptions. (See also Ridley, 1973.) Hoffman's (1961) otherwise pioneering study, which considered a woman's enjoyment of work an intervening variable in the effects of maternal employment on the child, included the father only in the form of a *control* for his occupation; the mother's behavior alone was assumed to shape the child's adjustment.

The absence of a systems perspective is particularly apparent here. A large number of interactions need to be put together. There is evidence that women's employment changes the division of labor in the home, although perhaps more so for blacks than whites (Aldous, 1969a) and not for higher income or professional couples (Paloma and Garland, 1971). It may increase women's dominance (Blood and Wolfe, 1960; Blood and Hamblen, 1968; Heer, 1958), especially over economic issues, although not necessarily over traditionally female areas like child-rearing (Middleton and Putney, 1960), and especially for work-committed women (Safilios-Rothschild, 1970). In two-worker families, both parents' self-awareness around the children and child care may increase with the husband's shift work (especially in lower middle-class families) and both the parents paying more attention to the children when home (Lein, 1974). If women work out of choice rather than necessity, furthermore, as many do, there is a happier marriage for both husbands and wives (Orden and Bradburn, 1969).

At the same time, a man's relation to *his* work may affect the quality of the husband-wife relationship when the wife works (Bailyn, 1970), his availability and willingness to do household chores and spend time with the children (Gerstl, 1961), and the emotional issues he brings to child-rearing (McKinley, 1964). His feelings about having a more dominant than traditional wife are also important; Lein's studies of two-worker families documented at least three patterns of husbands' responses based on their own backgrounds, community attitudes, and work situations (Lein et al., 1974). Although studies show that husbands of working wives may be liberal and not threatened (Axelson, 1963), there may also be additional conflict in the marriage (Nye and Hoffman, 1963: 272, 324), perhaps because there are two people ready to speak out and fight, as well as two more independent spouses. Mortimer, Hall, and Hill (1976) have proposed research that considers a husband's occupation as a *structural* constraint affecting his involvement in the family, thus helping to shape the opportunity structure for married women: whether or not they work and at what kinds of jobs. More research on such social structural issues is warranted, since present analyses are heavily weighted toward defining the husband's response to a working wife primarily in terms of male role ideology (e.g., Pleck, 1975).

Thus, to study *only* the husband or, more likely, *only* the wife, is to miss a set of interactions that may be critical for shaping the quality of interactions in the family. Bailyn found that a combination of wives' and husbands' orientations to both family and career predicted the happiness (by self-report) of their marriage. The marriages of career-oriented men and work-integrated women were not very happy. *Conventional* marriages of career-oriented men and traditional wives were happy to the extent that the base separation of interests were minimized and in lower income brackets. *Coordinate* marriages of work-integrated women and family-oriented men were happier when housework and child care were shared and income high (Bailyn, 1970). (See also Bailyn, 1973 and Rapoport, Rapoport, and

Thiessen, 1974, for studies of the effects of couple symmetry on enjoyment.) A total system approach will also be extremely important in studying a phenomenon likely to increase in the future: what happens to family relations when a woman *changes* her work (e.g., when a housewife takes a paying job)? (Studies indicate that times of transition are likely to make a woman more vulnerable to depression; Weissman and Paykel, 1974.)

Women's Contribution to Family Status

A fourth traditional assumption underlying investigation in this area has been pointed out by feminist critics of stratification research: that the husband's occupation alone supposedly defines class and status for the family (Haug, 1973; Acker, 1973). A woman's work and the material conditions of *her* life were generally considered irrelevant to class analysis and, secondarily then, to family dynamics. This stems from the more basic assumptions, repeated often in the literature but particularly attributed to Parsonian analysis (Parsons, 1949) that the family as a whole shares a status and that the man is the link with the economic system. There are many bases on which this should be challenged, and a challenge is as important for understanding social class and class-linked behavior in America as for producing a less ideological picture of women. Indeed recent research on 566 married working women from 1960 and 1970 national surveys showed that they do *not* derive their class position and identification exclusively or predominantly from the occupational positions of their husbands. The wives derived their own class identification based on *their* occupation even when the researchers controlled for the effects of the wife's father's occupational status and the wife having higher occupational status than the husband (Ritter and Hargens, 1975).

There is other evidence that the family's *unitary* position in the stratification system may be a little mythical, at least from the perspective of class-linked behavior. Bennett Berger's (1960) study of auto workers in suburbia showed the husbands retaining so-called working-class behaviors and attitudes much more fully and firmly than the wives, who already, after only two years, were behaving like middle-class suburbanites. This is not so surprising if one sees that the experiences of *all* family members —some joint, some independent—shape their behaviors and attitudes. If the men's working-class orientations are shaped by their factory work, then the women's can be influenced by the material conditions of *their* existence as suburban housewives. To which overall social class do such families belong? Tallman and Morgner (1970) found a range of differences between urban and suburban blue-collar families, indicating (unlike Berger's study) that the suburban families adopted life-styles more strongly resembling those of the middle class. However, they also saw that the husbands and wives adapted to suburban residence very differently and that it was often the *wives'* behavior that made the families look middle class. (Bernard, 1972, has made a similar point in her argument that there are "his" and "hers" marriages.) Hurvitz (1964) identified discrepancies in "class values" as a possible source of strain in blue-collar families: Wives may adopt middle-class values as a result of media exposure and then develop self-deprecating and husband-deprecating feelings.

There is also evidence that men of different classes are more divergent in some family behaviors, such as discipline techniques than women of different classes, who are closer together in their responses (McKinley, 1964; Gecas and Nye, 1974). We can invoke a similar explanation. The men's material conditions and the occupational experiences that shaped their world view vary greatly from class to class, while the women (housewives in this case) shared a much more similar "occupational milieu" despite the differences in their husbands' work. Caplow noted the dramatic similarity of working conditions for housewives of all social classes.

> With the passage of time, housewives have come to be the only large group in the population engaged in the same activity, and their work and working conditions have become even more the same with urbanization and with the diffusion of middle-class values ...
> (creating) an occupational culture of remarkable uniformity in which not only the technics but the values are effectively standardized. This identity of metier transcends class lines and regional boundaries. It is very different from the specialization which distributes the rest of the adult population into partially insulated compartments. (1954: 266.)

It would be very interesting to see what would be found if the joint effects of husbands' and wives' work were examined. How does the family behave if the whole family income would put the family in a different "class" than the husband's occupation taken alone? What happens if a wife's occupation would put her in a different social class with a different subculture and values than her husband's, as in the case of wives of blue-collar workers employed in white-collar jobs? There is evidence that class or status discrepancies in origin can generate strain (Pearlin, 1975). What about these discrepancies in present activities? Do the behaviors and attitudes of family members in such situations reflect the combination of classes? There are several logical possibilities: (a) the man's class dominates, (b) the woman's class dominates, (c) the higher class dominates, (d) the lower class dominates, or (e) a true combination. The analysis could also be extended to *children's* work. Children may bring important class- or status-discrepant experiences into the family through school work (e.g., Wilson, 1959). *How* differences are resolved is an important process question; whether and how the family constitutes a stratification unit is an important structural question.

Family Supports for Working Women

As with research on men, in this area too the great bulk of investigation considers the impact of work on the family and not interactions of effects in the other direction. Most research deals only with *men's* adjustment to the work setting. However, in the case of women, it *is* assumed that personal ties do affect work performance and work systems—all negatively because of women's strong family obligations. There is a grain of truth behind this stereotype, but only a grain. A study of successful women executives found that they minimized their personal relations during the "climbing" phase of their career and then tended to marry rather late in life, after they were clearly on their way to the top (Hennig, 1970). However, other research shows that marriage may not affect the productivity of professional women. Rapoport and Rapoport (1971) found two strategies for child-bearing in their studies of employed women in two career families: one, to have children early and resume work while still young and vigorous; the other, to establish the career first and facilitate the family building process through having more material resources and job perquisites.

The other side of the family-work connection has generally not been investigated for women: the ways in which family and other personal relations can contribute or not to work effectiveness for women. Research is now just beginning on the support systems of working women and how they can function to help a woman overcome the inevitable crises and frustrations she will face—particularly when she is in a stressful occupational situation, such as a rare woman in a traditionally male-dominated field (Kanter, 1977: Chapter 8). Weissman and Paykel conclude from their intensive investigations of depressed women that:

> While working at an interesting job might contribute significantly to a woman's self-respect, a job for which she was either under- or over-qualified, or one that was overwhelming, multiplied her chores and contributed to futility. . . . Women with few qualifications found that the outside job did not broaden horizons but only deepened calluses. . . . If no assistance was offered her at home, she eventually felt overworked and resentful. (1974:75.)

Recent research indicates that spouses are a less common source of help for working women than for men, but that women are more likely to use relatives. Blue-collar women tend to have the least primary and nearby supports, compared with both white-collar women and men of all classes (Warren, 1975), although husbands of women in lower middle-class jobs vary in their supportiveness and sharing of child care—rather likely—and housework—less likely—(Lein, 1974). Husbands of successful professional women, on the other hand, may be favorably disposed toward their wives' careers and translate this into concrete acts of support (Holmstrom, 1972). In other professional couples the wife may still be stuck with the bulk of the housework (Poloma and Garland, 1971). These issues are of critical importance to working women today, and they help account for how women manage to reconcile work and family roles (Epstein 1970).

The importance of the "wife role" in the success of managerial and professional men has often been discussed (although under-investigated in detail), but whether husbands can also help their wives' careers has not been a subject of inquiry, perhaps because of the assumptions I have described. However, studies of two-career families do highlight the benefits of colleagueship for the wife as well as the husband (Rapoport and Rapoport, 1971; Holmstrom, 1972). The personal conditions favoring the work effectiveness and successful work adjustment of women should be given equal consideration to that for men in research and policy formation. Organizational supports should also be considered; flexible working hours (see pp. 34-36) seem to be an innovation of particular benefit to women, while also extremely useful for men (Kanter, 1976a, 1977; Stein, Cohen, and Gadon, 1976; Racki, 1975).

The work-family connection, then, has been understood in a very different way for women than for men. Traditional assumptions about women's work and family roles have acted as blindfolds, preventing researchers from seeing some major distinctions that were more easily made in the case of working men. With the increased participation of women in the paid labor force, it becomes even more important to pose new research questions and to challenge conventional assumptions about women's work orientations, the work-family connection for women, and the family as a unit in social stratification.

A Social-Psychological Perspective: Working and Loving as Processes

From a process-oriented perspective, it is possible to examine the degree of *convergence* of work and family norms, rather than to continue to assume opposition and separation. The traditional Parsonian view of work-family separation held that universalistic, specific, emotionally neutral, and performance-oriented norms dominate the work world, whereas particularistic, diffuse, emotional, and quality- (or ascription) oriented norms dominate the family. Few people would accept this as a statement of anything more than the most ideal of types, for in the organizational world at least, a large body of research has been devoted to uncovering the particularistic, emotional, and ascriptive aspects of even apparently "rational" occupational systems. Caplow pointed out that a culture's myths and society's institutions are not identical, and thus, "the incompatibility between the occupational and family systems in operation is not really as sharp as Parsons' theoretical analysis would lead us to suppose" (1954:258).

What if we look at work and intimacy for a moment as processes or modes of organizing experience rather than as separate structures or activities? Differentiating the instrumental and expressive realm as two poles on a single continuum, Parsonian analysis was forced to conclude that the two modes or functions had to be assigned to separate institutions and within an institution to separate people. Critics, on the other hand, have pointed out that a more plausible case can be made for the ability of people to behave both instrumentally and expressively, making it clear that they constitute two different modes rather than ends of a single dimension (Slater, 1961). Indeed, Freud said that both work and love were requirements for the healthy person; work grounds people in the particulars of time and space, while love brings them into contact with the transcendent and universal.*

If we view "work" as the means by which people learn to mobilize for the accomplishment of tasks and "intimacy" as the way people orient themselves to one another, and if we further recognize that *both* tasks and relationships occur in both the occupational and family sectors, then we can also see the potential for the norms of one realm to converge with the *norms of the similar process* in the other realm. That is, the ways people accomplish tasks and respond to "production" in the family can be highly congruent with the ways these occur in the occupational world. (Indeed, contemporary Marxist scholars have argued that the family *is* a production as well as a consumption unit, producing labor power by producing maintenance services for present and future workers.) And similarly, the ways people orient themselves to one another at work can be highly congruent with the ways those individuals orient and express themselves in the intimate realm. Thus, the "instrumental" portion of family life is as likely as that of occupations to contain impersonal performance-oriented standards. And the "expressive" portion of organizations—the fact that they consist of individuals forming relationships—is as likely to contain particularistic, emotional elements as in the family.

What may vary from society to society is the number of activities defined in terms of "work" or "intimacy" orientations. In more traditional societies, intimacy orientations may prevail in the productive sphere to a much greater extent; production may

*Note that the Freudian association of work with the particular and love with the universal is directly opposite to the Parsonian assumption that the modern workplace is guided by universal*ism* and the family by particular*ism*. (I am indebted to an anonymous reviewer for this observation.)

be seen more in terms of interpersonal relationships, than in terms of tasks with impersonal performance standards. But even so, some work orientations occur around the organization and performance of tasks. In contemporary American society, work orientations may come to dominate a large portion of family life, because of the society's emphasis on work rather than intimacy ethics.

With this perspective, then, the *convergence* of some norms and orientations of the workplace and the household become clear. The tendency to define as much of domestic life as possible in terms of work or tasks with performance standards and orientations resembling those in organizations has grown since the 1800s. Around the turn of the century, the home economics movement and feminist critics argued for the "rationalization" of domestic labor, using examples of the efficiencies generated in industry. The words *science* and *economics* were used frequently, and analogies drawn to the factory. Jane Addams, writing in the first volume of the *American Journal of Sociology* in 1896, called domestic labor (as seen by servants) a "belated industry" which had not yet adapted to modern conditions, even though more and more household products were being prepared in outside kitchens. Addams saw women employers or servants resisting the modernization of housework in the same way that skilled craftsmen resisted the coming of machine technology. Charlotte Perkins Gilman (1903) went beyond the plight of the domestic servant to argue that all housework would be better performed and women's equality better secured if much domestic work was turned over to central organizations. And Richardson (1929:21) had this to say about the housewife as an "administrator."

The terms management and administration used interchangeably in the home are borrowed from business and industry and have much the same meaning in this new relationship. The well-ordered home of today, like other efficient enterprises, is run according to accepted principles of good management, even though the objectives for homemaking are human satisfactions and development rather than increased production or sales. . . . Homemaking . . . has remained, for the majority, a composite occupation, where the homemaker is both a worker and a manager, planning the daily routine and carrying out these plans.

But even though most housework has remained private and privately "managed," it is interesting to note that "industrial" standards were applied and continue to be applied to activities in the family sector: today, for example, in the wages-for-housework debate and the growing emphasis on time-limited, highly specific marriage "contracts."

What are some ways in which work norms and orientations enter family life? "Bureaucracy" or "rational organization" can be seen as a way of responding to activities rather than as a set of formal structures, as I have argued in defining a nursery school as phenomenologically "bureaucratic" (Kanter, 1972b); in this sense, families can easily resemble work organizations if they include experimentally similar elements. There are several possibilities for the carryover of occupational norms and orientations to the family:

1. through an emphasis on performance of discrete tasks as an indication of membership and contribution;

2. measurement of performance by "objective" standards derived from more universalistic and impersonal notions of minimum and ideal performance (e.g., grades in school, frequency of intercourse, number of orgasms, amount on paychecks, and spotlessness of the house;

3. rewards and contributions controlled by each person given or withheld depending on performance;

4. achievement (on discrete tasks) rather than intrinsic qualities as the measure of the person;

5. an expectation of "more" (goods, services, rewards, comforts) with increasing seniority;

6. and a legitimate ability to "fire" or "trade in" spouses if they do not meet standards.

There are other indications of an infusion of norms of the industrial and post-industrial era into middle-class families: "participatory democracy" in the form of family councils and joint decision making; parents becoming more like modern managers in the way they handle authority than patriarchs and matriarchs; shared tasks assigned to or rotated among children (and perhaps parents) according to a posted schedule, etc. Social critics have already commented frequently on the tendency of Americans to "work hard" at leisure or play. R. D. Laing has even argued that the family is the *most* "bureaucratic" modern institution in insisting on performance standards and the repression of feeling (see Kanter, 1974). How widespread these things are or what consequences they have for family life remain to be investigated. Riesman and Bloomberg (1957) made a similar point in arguing that work and leisure are becoming increasingly indistinct, because of the growing importance of interpersonal relations in each, reminiscent of pre-industrial styles. (Leisure, they predict, may become what workers recover from at work, as children recover from vacations at school.)

If premises of the modern organizational world carry over into some ways families define and organize work, the opposite analogy can also be drawn. Values drawn from family life, as a mode of intimacy or relationship orientations, carry over into the occupational-organizational worlds. This has been recognized before. Joan Aldous (1969) remarked that the supposed contrast between family and occupational roles was overdrawn, because of the known intrusion of interpersonal factors circumventing the formal job structure. She concludes that the "highly charged affective relations found in the family are also present in the occupational world and influence what goes on there, from job selection to job performance" (1969:707). Caplow (1954) wrote:

Emotional and affective elements do not enter into the work life. The evaluation of workers is always based—at least in part—on the same qualities which figure in the family role, even though these may not have the same value for occupational purposes. In many situations, factors irrelevant to functional purpose are dominant in the evaluation of performance. . . . Moreover, rational evaluation of performance is not necessarily alien to the scale of familial values. For a foreman, a teacher, or a private secretary, the quality of personal relations is a major component of efficiency. (1954:258.)

This argument reflects something more than the tendency social psychiatrists have noted for individuals to "project" family relations on work peers (such as seeing fathers in bosses) or to allow emotional problems to affect work relations; it holds that the very operation of an organization as a whole may reflect intimacy-derived patterns of relationships. Familial metaphors can be appropriately applied to several kinds of occupational relationships. Secretaries and their managers may have "office marriages" (see Kanter 1975, 1977); workers may be treated as though they were children; the founder of a new organization may act out the father role (Stein and Kanter, in progress). But even beyond such analogies, the norms of the intimate realm may spill over into workplaces.

The carryover of the "human" or "expressive" or "intimate" side of life into organizations is most evident in jobs involving human

75

contact. Many analysts have noted the resistance of service occupations to bureaucratization and even the tensions between administrators interested primarily in task organization and those who deliver services and thus allow intimate orientations to intrude. Gartner and Riessman (1974) have argued that there is a new work ethic in the making due to the expansion of the service sector, with its people-serving, relational ethos. Such an ethic may function to reintroduce or reinforce familial kinds of relationships and familial norms in the occupational world.

If there are tensions between work and intimacy, then, they do *not* revolve around occupations and families as separate institutions, for we have seen that work orientations can be important in the family sector and intimate orientations in the occupational sector. The family does not own intimacy any more than the occupational-organizational world owns work, although the family may be the principal realm in which intimacy norms are established and the organizational world the principal realm in which work norms are established. There may be considerable convergence between the processes and roles of the two sectors (taking into account, of course, the apparent differences that size of unit and type of activity create). Any tensions between work norms and intimacy norms may reside in the nature of these two human processes themselves, in the orientations required for love and work. Attempts to segregate them by defining them as belonging to separate institutions seem impossible to implement, since both reflect processes that will inevitably occur in any human system. Yet, this analysis can be taken as an opportunity to examine the *consequences* of the various ways love and work may be combined. Some modes of loving and working may be maximally conflictful; others maximally harmonious. For example, the performance-centered family norms outlined earlier may so ground a family in work that love becomes more difficult. In any case, segregation of institutions is not the answer.

Looking at the possible convergences between American work and family norms and treating work and intimacy as processes rather than structures alone can lead to a number of compelling research questions.

1. What cultural or ideological congruence has there been between developments in the nature of occupational and family processes? How have images of desirable conduct moved from

each sector into the other in American history?

2. For whom in the society are work and intimate sectors *most* separate and *least* separate? They are probably most separate for people in repetitive occupations with limited human contact whose families have strong cultural traditions—i.e., factory workers of recent immigrant background. It is these people for whom work is not an important life interest, who respond to the organization in terms of technology rather than people (Dubin, 1956) and whose family behavior is most traditional and least reflective of the norms of positions they occupy at work. On the other hand, work and intimacy are probably *least* separate for people in involving and high human contact jobs whose families want to be up-to-date and thus adopt values from recent social consensus. Here we would expect the most spillover between family and work. Other degrees of work-family intersection falling between these extremes could also be identified. Note that these styles are defined *both* by work type *and* family culture.

3. What are the consequences of varying degrees of separation and kinds of separation? How do different work-family patterns of separation and connectedness affect each system and the people in them? It has been often suggested that the development of children is impaired by their inability to see their parents at work; this proposition and others could be tested. On the other hand, how does it affect the operations of a work system if families of workers (e.g., wives and children of managers) can enter freely and families are barely separated from the workplace? How does it affect families? How do "colleague marriages" work?

4. What do *individuals* bring home of their jobs, and what do they bring to work of their families? How does this vary with work type and family culture? What difference does it make if what is carried over is hidden, indirect, or denied as opposed to open and direct? How do family systems of different kinds incorporate information, role tendencies, or stresses from the work sector, and how do they handle change that enters from changes at work? How do organizations incorporate information, role tendencies, or stresses from the family sector, and how do they handle change that enters from changes in private life? What happens when family members bring in different pressures, demands, or learnings stemming from different work situations? What happens when organization members bring in different

pressures, demands, or learnings stemming from different family situations?

5. What are the various ways work and intimacy may be combined in both workplaces and homes, and what are the consequences of each mode? What happens when the personnel are the same in both places—e.g., if people work with family members or become sexually involved with workmates?

6. A test of role theory: Do people tend to play the *same* or *different* kinds of informal roles in their occupations as in their families? Does this vary depending on the kinds of formal roles they are assigned in each sector and how congruent these formal roles are? For example, the wife of a small company president remarked that he communicates to her the same way he does to his staff: with hidden standards, concerns about loyalty, and outbursts of anger (Stein and Kanter, in progress). Another informant reported that her professor husband could not stop lecturing when he got home. In what other ways do people carry interpersonal orientations back and forth, regardless of the formal structure of the situation? How varied must the situation be for the person to play an entirely different role? Can people occupy quite distinctive positions in several social systems without letting one affect the other? What are the social and psychological mechanisms by which this is done?

7. Important questions can be raised about the limits of change in any one institution alone. Some people are members simultaneously of an occupational and a family system. Furthermore, some people carry over orientations and pressures from one into the other, in part because norms of the two sectors may converge. Thus, attempts to intervene in either system may be severely limited by the fact that some participants simultaneously hold membership in another system. Family therapists may be limited in their ability to effect change in a family alone if membership in work systems is also implicated. Pleck (1975) suggested a similar point in his identification of the current structure of the male occupational role as a limitation on sex role change in the family. Similarly, attempts to change the behavior of people in organizations may be limited by the fact that those people also belong to families. Such limitations require investigation. They also suggest that new conceptions of intervention to produce social change are in order, and that "problems" need to be located in several institutions—in all

systems in which participants have membership—rather than in only the one in which the "problems" are first identified. This means that organizations, especially, need to be more aware of, and accountable for, how their operations may affect the development of problems for members in other realms.

Now that a number of separate connections between work and family as structures and processes have been identified and a wide range of transactions between these realms identified, we can turn to an exploration of their joint effects on the personal well-being of individuals: their physical and mental health.

Work, Family, and Well-being:
The Need to View Joint Needs

The consequences for personal well-being of variations in social situations deserve considerable attention, and much effort has been devoted to this topic. There is theory and research asserting that work is essential to well-being; a body of research points to the physical and mental health consequences of work situations. There is another growing body of work on psychopathology in the family and the family as the generating milieu of some forms of mental illness and adjustment difficulties. However, there has been remarkably little attempt to link the two, that is, to locate problems in the work-family intersection, to determine the extent to which one system contributes to the health or illness possibilities of the other, or to discover what variations in each system make it most vulnerable to problems from the other.

Work and Well-being

There are a variety of arguments about the general importance of work for well-being. Work is a source of life purpose (Morse and Weiss, 1955), productivity (Price and Levinson, 1964), prized self-image (Wilensky, 1966), and validating experiences

81

(Rainwater, 1974), so that the absence of meaningful work is seen as a major source of personal disturbance. There is also evidence that job characteristics affect mental and physical health. In a well-validated study, Kornhauser (1962) found direct links between the skill and interest level of jobs in automotive manufacturing plants and the percentage of workers exhibiting "good" mental health; the relationship remained strong among men of very different personality types and pre-job backgrounds. Sales (1969) discovered an important way in which job demands could affect physical health. After laboratory studies and literature review, he concluded that overloading roles (i.e., a set of demands that could be met one by one but not in totality), especially coupled with low job satisfaction, were associated with coronary disease, as measured by serum cholesterol levels and heart rate. Kasl and French (1962) found that the skill level of a job can be associated with health indices, as measured by dispensary visits. Although they have no direct proof of the links, they argue that the association has to do with prestige and self-esteem effects. Continued employment and work satisfaction were correlated with high longevity, in another series of studies, and occupational groups differed in their "longevity quotients" (Palmore and Stone, 1973).

McLean and Taylor (1958) identified the psychic dilemmas and stresses of several occupational levels in organizations. As they rise, executives suffer loneliness, inadequacy feelings, and the negative consequences of stressful competition and constant change. (See also Eaton, 1967; Steiner, 1972.) As "men in the middle," first-line supervisors face conflicting pulls. The major stresses for hourly workers come from their powerless position on the bottom and the problems created by increased leisure, resulting either in boredom or the overload of a second job. McLean and Taylor also pointed out that alcoholism among workers has long been a major problem in industry. Kahn and French (1962), Kasl (1974), and House (1974) provide comprehensive reviews and theoretical formulations.

A number of state-and-rate studies have demonstrated strong associations between socioeconomic status and the incidence and type of mental illness. Hollingshead and Redlich (1958) found, for example, that the lower the social class (as measured by an index giving occupation the greatest weight), the greater the proportion of mental patients in the population over 24, controlling for sex, age, race, religion, and marital status, and with no evidence of a drift downward in class *because* of illness. Furthermore, they found that there were fewer neurotics and more psychotics as status decreased and that psychosomatic illnesses were inversely related to class. Alcoholism increased slightly as status decreased, rising sharply in the lowest social class. (See also Frumkin, 1955.) Brenner (1967, 1974) found that the rate of admissions to mental hospitals in New York State between 1910 and 1960 was inversely correlated with the state's employment index. Offering further proof that changes in job situation were associated with mental illness, he showed that the highest status ethnic groups (out of thirty-four) showed the most effects (since they had the most to lose from job displacement) and the lowest status (black and Puerto Rican) the least change in economic downturns. Bradburn and Caplovitz's (1965) studies of happiness provide confirming evidence on another issue. They found that the higher the income and socioeconomic status, the greater the reported happiness. The lower the socioeconomic status, the greater the prevalence of "uncontrollable worries." Occupational situation, then, both specifically and generally, plays a strong role in personal well-being.

Family Pathology

At the same time, the family's contribution to mental illness has been the subject of a growing body of literature and a relatively new profession, family therapy. Certain family characteristics and processes have been defined as pathology-generating, including scapegoating of a child by dissatisfied parents in a poor marital relationship (Vogel and Bell, 1967), "double-binding" communication that presents contradictory demands equally likely to elicit punishment if met (Bateson et al., 1956, 1963), apparent harmony masking confusion and disharmony (Wynne et al., 1958), and blurring of sex and generation boundaries (Lidz, 1963). Several of these theories contain biases and limits (see Mishler and Waxler, 1965, for a fine review), but they attest to the growth of interest in the role of family dynamics in personal well-being. Critics such as R. D. Laing and his colleagues have tried to generalize such theories beyond severe instances of symptom formation to an indictment of the role of seemingly "normal" families in the distresses experienced by members while involved in that family or, in the case of the family of orientation, in later life (Kanter, 1974).

What is striking about these formulations is the almost total absence of attention to the family's social situation or, given the interest of this paper, in the work situation of family members as sources of stress that affect family dynamics and hence well-being. Variables from outside the family system rarely enter into consideration; the family appears in such analyses as a closed system. Indeed, the father (for many families the principal participant in the occupational system) hardly appears in many accounts of pathological families; he is noted primarily by his psychological absence. Fromm-Reichman's identification in 1948 of the "schizophrenogenic mother" produced a flurry of studies on the centrality of the mother in a child's pathology and general agreement that the father was peripheral, even though when the father is described, the characteristics vary from passive and ineffectual to harsh and dominating (Check, 1965). Yet a careful reading of case studies of "pathological" families (e.g., Henry, 1965; Parker, 1972; Laing and Esterson, 1964; Esterson, 1970) can reveal the ways in which occupational variables are, in fact, entering into the family's situation. Even if the principal role of work *is* the removal of the father from effective interaction in the family, external influences are still affecting the family's internal possibilities. Bettleheim and Sylvester (1950) have argued that at the very least a father's job may provide symbolic material for an emotionally disturbed child.

It is critical to bridge the gap between knowledge of the stress-producing aspects of work situations and of family systems. How tension and illness-producing features of one system affect the likelihood of a member's successful adjustment to the other system is important to know, especially if we are to extend our understanding of the barriers to well-being in our society and the ability of helpers to intervene to produce greater levels of health. A few investigations of executive life-styles have noted the negative effects of corporate positions on the well-being of the family, especially on members other than the executive himself. To recapitulate: Culbert and Renshaw (1972) have noted the family stress produced by executive travel. Weissman and Paykel found moving—a common feature of corporate life—to be a cause of depression in women; Levinson (1964) presents anecdotal evidence that unwanted babies are produced by wives forced to move against their inclination. Inordinate time demands, pressure to pursue careers singlemindedly, and a growing gap in the situations and learning opportunities of husbands and wives may contribute to alcoholism and depression in wives, marital infidelity, divorce, and symptoms of personal pathology (Levinson, 1964; Seidenberg, 1973; Cuber and Harroff, 1965). Many of these writers suggest that health-promoting interventions in situations, such as these, must occur *in the work-family interface*. And I suggest that it may also be appropriate to look at the intersection of the two systems in a much wider range of instances of mental and physical stress.

Needed Links

Connections that have been made in social science research thus far, as I have already indicated, have tended to consider the impact of generalized occupational status on well-being in the family realm. In much of this work, occupational status (or social class, measured largely by occupational status) was used as a global variable and associated with a simple output measure in the family, such as marital satisfaction—a prime example of concern with "states and rates." A large body of literature identified the inverse correlations between socioeconomic status and divorce or marital dissatisfaction (e.g., Weeks, 1942-1943; Nimkoff, 1943; Hollingshead, 1950; Williamson, 1952; Monahan, 1955; Goode, 1956; Bernard, 1966; Hicks and Platt, 1970; Renne, 1970). There have been some attempts to specify the nature of the association more precisely. The relationship between socioeconomic status and satisfaction appears stronger for blacks than whites (Bernard, 1966; Renne, 1970). Divorce rates can vary considerably by occupation, even within the same status level. For example, Monahan (1955) found that the rate was higher for cooks than barbers, taxi drivers than truck drivers, physicians than dentists, and teachers than engineers. (See also Nimkoff, 1943; Udry, 1966.)

Further identification of the effects of occupational characteristics (as opposed to status) on marital dynamics and individual well-being in the family has not been attempted, although it would seem critical to recognize that the *effects of work might vary considerably*, even within the same formal occupational category, and that *how these situations affect the family depends on the nature of the family system*.

Goode (1956) was one of the few scholars to point out that the impact of economic factors on families would depend on the meaning assigned to them by the family. It would also seem important to examine family process and dynamics in order to understand how stresses introduced by occupational situations are handled by families. During the depression, Angell (1936) showed that families' adjustment to economic strain caused by unemployment or a severe drop in income depended on the nature of the family system (see also Cavan, 1959). Relatively problem-free and symptom-free adjustment tended to occur when roles were flexible and life philosophy was not dominated by materialism. Koos's (1946) later studies of how adequately low income families coped with "troubles" (non-routine stress) highlighted these and other family-system variables, including the family's sense of direction and willingness of members to accept and act upon some common definition of what would be "good" for the whole unit. It is interesting to note that in both sets of studies families that coped well were often not as strongly patriarchal as those that did not, despite the greater expected frequency of traditional families during that period. Economic trouble could make the father seem a failure as a breadwinner, causing him to lose authority. If the family did not already have the basis for role flexibility, for pulling together, and for valuing people beyond economic contribution, then the result of such loss of paternal authority was likely to be stress and poor adjustment —a vacuum that no one else could fill. Journalistic accounts of the effects of job loss during the recent economic crises also indicate that how a couple cope is a function of the kind of system they had previously established (Stevens, 1975): flexible or inflexible, based on personal affection or based on economic exchange.

New theories of family process, generated largely by family therapists, can provide a key to the kinds of concepts necessary to understand how economic variables enter and affect different kinds of families. Kantor's and Lehr's (1975) provocative distinction between closed, open, and random system families is one such promising theory. Open system families would appear to be the most flexible in adapting to stresses introduced by the work system.

The simple state-and-rate associational studies pose additional problems beyond a lack of specification of differential family styles. They have no way of taking into account how the *meaning* (and thus potential impact) of work variables changes with a changing occupational situation. Different aspects of work life become salient as the work situation itself changes; one of the effects of location in the occupational system is a differential set of assumptions, worries, and concerns. How economic strain affects the well-being of families also depends on the family members' past and anticipated future economic and occupational situation. *Absolute* income level is one important variable, for loss of income affects high and low income families very differently even at the same relative proportion of loss, as another depression study makes clear (Conrad, 1939). *Duration* of situation is also important. People who hold menial jobs temporarily but anticipate future change may not show the same effects as those for whom poor working conditions appear indefinite. *Opportunities* rather than present situation is the important variable (Kanter, 1977: Chapter 6). Depression families that can define unemployment as temporary and as caused by systemic rather than personal failures may show few of the negative effects of unemployment manifested by those for whom it is a chronic situation; previous location in the economic system, of course, affects these perceptions.

In looking at the impact of work variables on well-being, then, we need to identify which aspects have the greatest importance at different levels and for people in different situations. For the very poor, the mere fact of employment versus unemployment may be the most critical stress-producing variable: whether a family member has the prospects to produce a secure source of income and who those family members are. Rainwater (1970) and others have pointed out that for ghetto blacks the fact that women rather than men have greater opportunity to bring in secure income helps define one form of family life—the woman-headed household—or a series of family "problems" and indications of stress (such as high separation rates). (We must be careful, however, not to use middle-class values to impute "pathology" to such families, for, as Rodman, 1963, 1964, pointed out, such patterns may in fact represent highly successful adjustment to economic realities.) Security versus insecurity may be the most relevant variable for people in this situation. (See also Miller, 1964a.) As income becomes less of an issue, however, then other aspects of the work situation become more salient: relative status, occupational milieux, job pressures, and so forth.

If we were better able to specify which aspects of occupational life are most stress-producing for people in different occupational situations, we would be in a better position to refine and understand the simple state-and-rate associations between economic variables and family strain. We might then also be able to explain certain conflicting findings that occur when the same simple association is tested under slightly different circumstances. It is not clear, for example, only from the research to date, for which people job satisfaction is a major correlate of family satisfaction. Williamson (1952) found that "occupational adjustment" and job satisfaction had only borderline significance in association with marital satisfaction. Bradburn and Caplovitz (1964) argued that job tension and marriage tension tended to go hand-in-hand, but they also found some independence in the two measures of satisfaction. But Dyer (1964) found that for blue-collar workers, "in some cases job satisfaction, or the lack of it, seems to be the factor of primary importance influencing the whole tenor of family life" (1964:86). One explanation for this difference lies in the occupational milieux. In Dyer's study, it was the fact that the workers in question lived in a college town where they were made very aware of the low prestige of their jobs, and they worked in small businesses or home-based operations which made wives a major source of influence on their husbands' jobs. Other studies of blue-collar workers, in contrast, have tended to look at those workers in larger, more routinized, more mechanized jobs; the wives of such workers tended to feel isolated and left out of the husband's job (e.g., Rainwater, Coleman, and Handel, 1959; Sexton, 1964), but marital tension was not necessarily a function of husband's job satisfaction rather than wife's isolation. These studies make clear that the relationship between work strain and family strain is not a simple one, unlike the image presented by state-and-rate analysis, but rather depends on an interaction between the *specific* occupational and family milieux.

A needed next step, then, in research and policy on personal well-being, is to consider the *joint* effects of work and family system memberships. To ask what kinds of work situations maximize and minimize the prospects for family well-being and what kinds of personal-familial arrangements maximize and minimize the prospects for well-being at work are only first questions. We must go further and consider the likely interaction of work situation and family dynamics. Some things that are fine by themselves are lethal in combination. What kinds of families are most vulnerable to stresses introduced by the nature of the occupational worlds with which members interact? How does personal stress-producing work affect the lives of other people close to the worker, and how is this mediated by those others' own work situations? How do strained family processes affect the prospects for satisfying work life, for people in different kinds of occupational situations, for women as well as men?

Finally, to raise a larger policy question pervading this review, what is the responsibility of the institutions in which work takes place for the personal and familial consequences of work conditions and work arrangements? To some extent, other family members are "innocent victims" of stresses produced at work and of organizational policies that directly or indirectly constrain their own full development as individuals and as a joint human system. At the same time, workers themselves are sometimes penalized at work for strains they carry with them from disturbances in the intimate realm. *Can organizations more fully and responsibly take into account their inevitable interface with the personal lives of their participants?* This may be a major social welfare issue of the decades to come.

I have argued throughout this report that work and family are connected in many subtle and unsubtle, social, economic, and psychological ways belying the simplified version of the myth of separate worlds with which I began. If anything, the literature surveyed here makes evident the fact that separateness itself might be seen as a variable and a dimension, rather than a fixed aspect of social structure. We need to pay attention to the variety of *patterns* of separateness and connectedness between working and loving, occupations and families, in the United States. And we need to examine the consequences of these patterns of work-family association for the lives of American men, women, and children.

A large number of research topics have been defined throughout this report. From a policy standpoint, some would appear to be more urgent than others. For example, there is already a large body of evidence linking low income and marginal labor force position to various indices of family "disruption." Whatever one's definition of "normal" family life and optimal individual development, it is at least clear that poor economic position places undue stress on personal relations. There would seem to be little need to further document this association. However, it would be valuable in an area, such as this, to specify the conditions under which people cope most effectively with stresses introduced into their lives by work conditions, so that people can be supported in their *own* attempts to create satisfying lives. An emphasis on coping mechanisms, rather than only documenting statistical associations, would help alleviate the assumption of "pathology" introduced into discussions of the family life of the disadvantaged in the 1960s. We would learn about the sources of personal strength which social policy can help reinforce. Research, in short, should not contribute to foreclosing the options for people's private arrangements by assuming only a limited number of "healthy" or permissible life-styles.

Five areas stand out as priorities for research and theory.

1. *Patterns of work-family connection and the characteristic benefits, costs, and dilemmas associated with each.*

Work and family are separated or connected in many different ways for people in this society, but the consequences of each pattern are not well-known. Social critics of the past decade often pointed out the negative effects (especially on housewives and children) of the extreme separation of work and family in some occupations. But there may be advantages as well as costs, for some people, under some conditions, to a degree of separation of home life and work life. At the same time, highly integrated conditions (such as small family businesses) may bear their own particular possibilities for stress as well as benefits to the family. Models need to be developed, and they need to be proposed in terms of *dilemmas*—the kinds of situations that must be managed within each pattern. Social organization does not automatically determine human responses, but it does set limiting conditions and confront people in various locations with characteristic sets of problems and choices. (An example of the dilemma approach is in the treatment of the corporate wife's career progression, reported on p. 29. See also Kanter, 1977.)

2. *Nepotism and anti-nepotism.*

The history and effects of anti-nepotism rules as well as the issues that arise when family members are employed in the same organization or work group would be a valuable research topic. Such questions arise particularly as the number of married women in the labor force continues to grow and as organizations experiment with new work patterns, such as "shared jobs."

3. *Occupational situations and organizational arrangements as structural constraints on personal and family development.*

Issues and questions have already been spelled out at length on pp. 23-51. Of particular importance as structural constraints are time and timing. Since time is a scarce resource, and families or personal priorities too often get what is "left over" after work, quantity of time and its scheduling can have a major impact on family life and private relationships. Research on this topic could also be integrated with new psychobiological and sociobiological investigation of temporal rhythms and other time effects.

A second critical area is the nature of occupational demands as constraints on personal life. More research on absorptive occupations is warranted. Threads from the important labor-leisure investigations of the 1950s and early 1960s should be picked up, with examination of a range of occupations and associated conditions within the family or personal life-styles. Those occupations that absorb people "negatively"—that is, "burn them out" and leave them with little energy for personal life— should also be examined.

4. *The effects of adult career development or work progression on personal and familial relations.*

How do people change in the course of their work experiences, and how do these changes facilitate or disrupt personal relations or constitute dilemmas that require resolution? The current wave of research on adult development should be encouraged to continue but with a special focus on work experiences and the attainment of new positions at work as "socializers" which may affect the ways people view and handle their marital, parental, or community roles. The effects of congruent or incongruent experiences among family members should also be investigated.

5. *Joint effects of work and family on disruptions of personal well-being.*

Wherever health or illness is considered in social context, it would be important to consider it as a joint outcome of participation in at least two systems: a system of family relations and a work system (in which some but not all family members, including the individual in question, participate). For example, as family psychotherapy continues to grow and family medicine gains prominence as a field, practitioners as well as researchers should also view the family (or the intimate system) in the context of its work location, organizational situation, and employment conditions. Practitioner training should include understanding of economic, organizational, and occupational stresses on individuals and families.

Social Policy Innovations and Experiments

There is also a need for policy experiments and research into their effects. A number of such innovations and interventions can be identified.

1. *Flextime (flexible working hours).*

Some of the benefits to flextime systems were identified on pp. 34-36. Flextime plans are growing in the United States (they are much more common in Europe), but they need further encouragement. In particular, the effects of increased temporal flexibility on personal life need to be researched, and if (as preliminary evidence suggests) the benefits to families, community and political participation, and the personal health and growth of individuals can be demonstrated, such benefits should be widely publicized in order to encourage further implementation of flexible time policies. Flextime would seem especially critical for married women with family responsibilities and for single parents. It might also help those who would like to care for the sick or the elderly within the family rather than in outside institutions.

2. *Organizational change and job redesign.*

If certain absorptive occupations unduly constrain personal and family life, and if certain low opportunity, low autonomy, and low skill occupations have negative effects on mental health and create a source of tension that may manifest itself in hostility within the family, then jobs need to be redesigned. For those in low opportunity, low autonomy situations, worker participation, job enrichment, and increased opportunities for job control and growth may be necessary not only to ensure equity in the workplace but also to generate greater satisfaction for the worker in the family context. Similarly, redefining "success" for those at the top and redesigning reward structures so as to discourage rather than to encourage "work-aholics" may be equally necessary for other families to prosper. In this connection, the effects of experimental kinds of organizations (such as work cooperatives, worker-controlled and managed firms, or nonhierarchical and decentralized firms) on personal and family relations should be investigated. The possibilities for change in the organization of work life in order to improve the quality of *all* life is an extremely high priority.

3. *Joint family and work-group meetings and workshops.*

In keeping with my assumption that policy should help people build their own strengths, another step would be to encourage the families of people in ongoing work units to meet together to define their own issues and develop their own solutions. At the very least, such occasional or routine meetings would help other family members feel included in and more knowledgeable about what the worker does at work, and it would help them build connections with others in a similar situation. At most, such meetings might result in policy suggestions to employers or a greater voice for workers and their families in organizational policies. Where these kinds of workshops have been conducted, they have tended to be extremely well received by workers and families, although many organizations are reluctant to sanction or support them. (One program with which I was associated brought together men in a high demand work unit who complained of tensions at home and their wives who increasingly felt excluded and distanced from their husbands. Though not all problems were solved, effective support systems were built for both parties.)

4. *Bringing children (and spouses) to work.*

On-work-site day care is a policy issue that others have dealt with at great length. Here it may be suggested only that the opportunity for children (and even excluded spouses) to share some time at workplaces with workers has potential value that should be investigated. Single parents, especially, might appreciate the opportunity to bring their children to work for part of the day.

5. *On-work-site counseling.*

More and more employing organizations are making some psychological as well as medical counseling available to people on the work site. How this opportunity affects personal out-of-work relations is still a question. Perhaps the value of this may lie in the recognition that personal crises can affect work life and need to be acknowledged, with supportive help provided. But the "paternalism" inherent in such a policy, issues of confidentiality and effects on careers, all raise uneasy questions that must be answered. And, if some stresses arise from the nature of jobs, it is important to ask whether the Band-Aid solution of counseling is really an adequate substitute for organizational reform or job redesign.

6. *Community supports for employed women.*

If one major issue for married employed women with children is managing their multiple involvements, attention needs to be given to community services that will provide aid and support, especially for single parents without familial supports and for working women whose husbands fail to give it to them.

7. *Leaves and sabbaticals.*

A wide variety of personal leaves and sabbaticals can be considered. Maternity and paternity leave are the most obvious, but beyond these, there are a number of situations in which career flexibility and the possiblility for brief "interruptions" could aid personal and family life.

8. *Workman's compensation for families of work "victims."*

Recent court decisions have extended workman's compensation to executives, managers, and other white-collar workers, as well as to widows whose husbands had fatal heart attacks in the course of executive pressures (Stessin, 1976). There are large implications here. The legal issues and financial costs of such extensions need to be investigated. The feasibility of allowing families in general to claim compensation (such as for the costs of psychotherapy to handle stresses introduced by work situations) should be examined. Such policies might also serve as a deterrent, forcing employers to make changes in family-stress-producing situations.

9. *"Family responsiblity statements" by organizations.*

The suggestion of a "family impact statement" attached to governmental legislation, which Vice President Mondale made while serving as a Senator, is still under review. However, as Gerzon (1973) pointed out, government programs, such as the Social Security Administration, have played a major role in shaping the environment for families and children. But perhaps another arena may be proposed: "family responsiblity statements" filed by employing organizations. If, as I suspect, the nature of the work world plays a dominant role in the possibilities for families and for personal satisfaction in out-of-work life, then the organizations in which most Americans work might begin to take some responsiblity for their effects on families and personal relations. Organizations could file a "family responsiblity" document in the same way as an affirmative action plan, although without much of the statistic-gathering and paper work that the latter entails. The statement could include a summary of major organizational policies (such as the timing of work, promotion practices, job control, and executive transfers) along with consideration of how they might affect families and how the organization intends to alleviate major stresses.

The human impact of work organizations—on the workers and on those related people linked to the organization through them—needs the full attention of policy makers.

References

Aberle, David F., and Kaspar Naegele, "Middle-Class Fathers'
    Occupational Role and Attitudes toward Children," *American
    Journal of Orthopsychiatry*, 22 (April 1952): 366–78.
Acker, Joan, "Women and Social Stratification: A Case of Intellectual
    Sexism," *American Journal of Sociology*, 78 (January 1973):
    936–45.
Adams, Bert N., and James E. Butler, "Occupational Status and
    Husband-Wife Social Participation," *Social Forces*, 46
    (June 1967): 501–7.
Addams, Jane, "A Belated Industry," *American Journal of Sociology*,
    1 (March 1896): 536–50.
Aldous, Joan, "Occupational Characteristics and Males' Role
    Performance in the Family," *Journal of Marriage and the Family*,
    31 (November 1969): 707–12.
Aldous, Joan, "Wives' Employment Status and Lower-Class Men as
    Husband-Fathers: Support for the Moynihan Thesis," *Journal of
    Marriage and the Family*, 31 (August 1969): 469–76.
Aldous, Joan, and Murray A. Straus, "Social Networks and Conjugal
    Roles: A Test of Bott's Hypothesis," *Social Forces*, 44 (June
    1966): 576–80.
Anderson, W. A., "Family Social Participation and Social Status
    Self-Ratings," *American Sociological Review*, 11 (June 1946):
    253–8.
Angell, Robert Cooley, *The Family Encounters the Depression*. New
    York: Charles Scribner's Sons, 1936.

Aronowitz, Stanley, *False Promises: The Shape of American Working Class Consciousness.* New York: McGraw Hill, 1973.

Axelson, Leland J., "The Marital Adjustment and Marital Role Definitions of Husbands of Working and Nonworking Wives," *Journal of Marriage and the Family,* 25 (May 1963): 189–195.

Bailyn, Lotte, "Career and Family Orientations of Husbands and Wives in Relation to Marital Happiness," *Human Relations,* 23 (1970): 97–113.

Bailyn, Lotte, "Family Constraints on Women's Work," *Annals of the New York Academy of Science,* 208 (March 1973): 82–90.

Bailyn, Lotte, "Involvement and Accommodation in Technical Careers: An Inquiry into the Relation to Work at Mid-Career," in J. Van Maanen (ed.), *Organizational Careers.* London: Wiley International, 1976.

Bailyn, Lotte, and Edgar Schein, "Life/Career Considerations as Indicators of Quality of Employment," in A. D. Biderman and T. F. Drury (eds.), *Measuring Work Quality for Social Reporting.* Beverly Hills, Calif.: Sage, 1976.

Bakke, E. Wight, *The Unemployed Worker: A Study of the Task of Making a Living without a Job.* New Haven, Conn.: Yale University Press, 1940.

Baltzell, E. Digby, *Philadelphia Gentlemen: The Making of a National Upper Class.* Glencoe, Ill.: Free Press, 1958.

Barnes, Louis B., and Simon A. Hershon, "Transferring Power in the Family Business," *Harvard Business Review,* 54 (July-August 1976): 105–14.

Bart, Pauline, "Portnoy's Mother's Complaint," *Trans-action,* 7 (November-December 1970): 69–74.

Bartemeier, Leo, "The Children of Working Mothers: A Psychiatrists' View," in National Manpower Council, *Work in the Lives of Married Women.* New York: Columbia University Press, 1958.

Bateson, Gregory, Don D. Jackson, Jay Haley, and John H. Weakland, "A Note on the Double Bind—1962," *Family Process,* 2 (March 1963): 154–61.

Bateson, Gregory, Don D. Jackson, Jay Haley, and John H. Weakland, "Toward a Theory of Schizophrenia," *Behavioral Science,* 1 (October 1956): 251–64.

Becker, Howard S., and James Carper, "The Elements of Identification with an Occupation," *American Sociological Review,* 21 (June 1956): 341–8.

Becker, Howard S., and Anselm L. Strauss, "Careers, Personality, and Adult Socialization," *American Journal of Sociology,* 62 (November 1956): 253–63.

Bell, Daniel, "The Break-Up of Family Capitalism," *The End of Ideology.* Rev. ed. New York: Collier Books, 1961.

Bell, Daniel, *The Coming of Post-Industrial Society: A Venture in Social Forecasting.* New York: Basic Books, 1973.

Bell, Robert R., "Lower Class Negro Mothers' Aspirations for Their Children," *Social Forces,* 43 (May 1965): 493–500.

Berg, Ivar, and David Rogers, "Former Blue-Collarites in Small Business," in A. Shostak and W. Gomberg (eds.), *Blue-Collar*

World: Studies of the American Worker. Englewood Cliffs, N.J.: Prentice-Hall, 1964.

Berger, Bennett M., *Working-Class Suburb: A Study of Auto Workers in Suburbia.* Berkeley: University of California Press, 1960.

Bernard, Jessie, *American Family Behavior.* New York: Harper, 1942.

Bernard, Jessie, *The Future of Marriage.* New York: World Publishing, 1972.

Bernard, Jessie, "Marital Stability and Patterns of Status Variables," *Journal of Marriage and the Family,* 18 (November 1966): 421–39.

Besner, Arthur, "Economic Deprivation and Family Patterns," in M. B. Sussman (ed.), *Sourcebook in Marriage and the Family.* 3rd ed. Boston: Houghton Mifflin, 1963.

Blau, Peter M., and Otis Dudley Duncan, with Andrea Tyree, *The American Occupational Structure.* New York: Wiley, 1967.

Blauner, Robert, *Alienation and Freedom.* Chicago: University of Chicago Press, 1964.

Blood, Robert O., Jr., and Robert L. Hamblin, "The Effect of the Wife's Employment on the Family Power Structure," *Social Forces,* 36 (May 1958): 347–52.

Blood, Robert O., Jr., and Donald M. Wolfe, *Husbands and Wives.* New York: Free Press, 1960.

Bowles, Samuel, and Herbert Gintis, *Schooling in Capitalist America.* New York: Basic Books, 1976.

Bradburn, Norman M., and David Caplovitz, *Reports on Happiness.* Chicago: Aldine, 1965.

Braverman, Harry, *Labor and Monopoly Capital.* New York: Monthly Review Press, 1974.

Brim, Orville G., Jr., "Socialization through the Life Cycle," in O. G. Brim, Jr., and S. Wheeler (eds.), *Socialization after Childhood.* New York: Wiley, 1966.

Brim, Orville G., Jr., and Ronald P. Abeles, "Work and Personality in the Middle Years," *Social Science Research Council Items,* 29 (September 1975): 29–33.

Brenner, Harvey M., "Economic Change and Mental Hospitalization: New York, 1910–1960," *Social Psychiatry,* 2 (1967): 180–88.

Brenner, Harvey M., *Mental Illness and the Economy.* Cambridge, Mass.: Harvard University Press, 1974.

Brofenbrenner, Urie, "Socialization and Social Class through Time and Space," in E. Maccoby, T. Newcomb, and R. Hartley (eds.), *Readings in Social Psychology.* New York: Holt, 1958.

Burchinal, Lee G., "Personality Characteristics of Children," in F. I. Nye and L. W. Hoffman (eds.), *The Employed Mother in America.* Chicago: Rand McNally, 1963.

Byington, Margaret F., "The Family in a Typical Mill Town," *American Journal of Sociology,* 14 (March 1909): 648–59.

Caplow, Theodore, *The Sociology of Work.* Minneapolis: University of Minnesota Press, 1954.

Carter, Hugh, and Paul C. Glick, *Marriage and Divorce: A Social and Economic Study.* Cambridge, Mass.: Harvard University Press, 1970.

Carter, Reginald, "The Myth of Increasing Non-Work vs. Work Activities," *Social Problems*, 18 (Summer 1970): 52–67.

Cavan, Ruth Shonle, *The American Family*. 4th ed. New York: Crowell, 1969.

Cavan, Ruth Shonle, "Unemployment: Crisis of the Common Man," *Marriage and Family Living*, 21 (May 1959): 139–46.

Charters, W. W., "How Much Do College Professors Work?" *Journal of Higher Education*, 6 (1942): 298–301.

Cheek, Frances E., "The Father of the Schizophrenic: The Function of a Peripheral Role," *Archives of General Psychiatry*, 13 (October 1965) 336–45.

Chilman, Catherine S., "Child-Rearing and Family Relationship Patterns of the Very Poor," in M. B. Sussman (ed.), *Sourcebook in Marriage and the Family*. 3rd ed. Boston: Houghton Mifflin, 1963.

Chinoy, Eli M., *Automobile Workers and the American Dream*. New York: Doubleday, 1955.

Clark, Alice, *Working Life of Women in the Seventeenth Century*. London: Frank Cass, 1968. (First published in 1919.)

Clark, James V., "Task Group Therapy (II): Intervention and Problems of Practice," *Human Relations*, 23 (October 1970): 383–403.

Clarke, Alfred C., "Leisure and Occupational Prestige," *American Sociological Review*, 21 (June 1956): 205–14.

Cohen, Allan R., Personal correspondence, 1975.

Cohen, Allan R., *Tradition, Change and Conflict in Indian Business*. The Hague: Mouton, 1974.

Conrad, Laetitia M., "Differential Depression Effects on Families of Laborers, Farmers, and the Business Class: A Survey of an Iowa Town," *American Journal of Sociology*, 44 (January 1939): 526–33.

Coser, Lewis M., *Greedy Institutions*. New York: Free Press, 1974.

Coser, Rose L. (ed.), *The Family: Its Structure and Functions*. New York: St. Martin's, 1974.

Cuber, John, with Peggy B. Harroff, *The Significant Americans: A Study of Sexual Behavior among the Affluent*. New York: Appleton-Century, 1965.

Culbert, Samuel A., and Jean R. Renshaw, "Coping with the Stresses of Travel as an Opportunity for Improving the Quality of Work and Family Life," *Family Process*, 11 (September 1972): 321–337.

Dalton, Melville, "Informal Factors in Career Achievement," *American Journal of Sociology*, 56 (January 1951): 407–15.

Davis, Allison, "The Motivation of the Underprivileged Worker," in W. F. Whyte (ed.), *Industry and Society*. New York: McGraw Hill, 1946.

Davis, Allison, and Robert J. Havighurst, "Social Class and Color Differences in Child-Rearing," *American Sociological Review*, 11 (December 1946). 698–710.

De Grazia, Sebastian, *Of Time, Work and Leisure*. New York: Twentieth Century Fund, 1962.

Demby, Emanuel, "Over-the-Counter Life-Style," *Psychology Today*, 5 (April 1972): 75–8, 110.

Dexter, Elisabeth Anthony, *Career Women of America, 1776-1840*. Francestown, N.H.: Marshall Jones, 1950.

Donald, Marjorie N., and Robert J. Havighurst, "The Meanings of Leisure," *Social Forces*, 37 (May 1959): 355–60.

Dotson, Floyd, "Patterns of Voluntary Association among Urban Working-Class Families," *American Sociological Review*, 16 (October 1951): 687–93.

Dubin, Robert, "Industrial Workers' Worlds," *Social Problems*, 3 (January 1956): 131–42.

Dubnoff, Steven, "The Family and Absence from Work: Irish Workers in a Lowell, Massachusetts, Cotton Mill, 1860." Unpublished paper, November 1975, Brandeis University, Waltham Mass.

Duncan, Beverly, and Otis Dudley Duncan, "Family Stability and Occupational Success," *Social Problems*, 16 (Winter 1969): 273–85.

Duncan, Otis Dudley, "Social Stratification and Mobility: Problems in the Measurement of Trend," in E. B. Sheldon and W. E. Moore (eds.), *Indicators of Social Changes: Concepts and Measurements*. New York: Russell Sage Foundation, 1968.

Dyer, William G., "A Comparison of Families of High and Low Job Satisfaction," *Marriage and Family Living*, 18 (February 1956): 58–60.

Dyer, William G., "Family Reactions to the Father's Job," in A. Shostak and W. Gomberg (eds.), *Blue-Collar World: Studies of the American Worker*. Englewood Cliffs, N.J.: Prentice-Hall, 1964.

Dyer, William G., "The Interlocking of Work and Family Social Systems among Lower Occupational Families," *Social Forces*, 34 (March 1956): 230–233.

Dyer, William G., "Parental Influence on the Job Attitudes of Children," *Sociology and Social Research*, 42 (January-February 1958): 203–206.

Dynes, Russell R., Alfred C. Clarke, and Simon Dinitz, "Levels of Occupational Aspiration: Some Aspects of Family Experience as a Variable," *American Sociological Review*, 21 (April 1956): 212–5.

Eaton, Merrill T., "Detecting Executive Stress in Time," *Industrial Medicine and Surgery*, 36 (February 1967): 115–8.

Elder, Glen H., Jr., *Children of the Great Depression: Social Change in Life Experience*. Chicago: University of Chicago Press, 1974.

Elder, Glen H., Jr., "Role Relations, Sociocultural Environments, and Autocratic Family Ideology," *Sociometry*, 28 (June 1965): 173–96.

Ennis, Philip H., "The Definitions and Measurement of Leisure," in E. B. Sheldon and W. E. Moore (eds.), *Indicators of Social Change: Concepts and Measurements*. New York: Russell Sage Foundation, 1968.

Epstein, Cynthia Fuchs, "Positive Effects of the Double Negative: Explaining the Success of Black Professional Women," *American Journal of Sociology*, 78 (January 1973): 912–35.

Epstein, Cynthia Fuchs, *Woman's Place: Options and Limits in Professional Careers*. Berkeley: University of California Press, 1970.

Esterson, Aaron, *The Leaves of Spring: A Study in the Dialectics of Madness*. London: Tavistock, 1970.

Farber, Bernard, *Kinship and Class: A Midwestern Study*. New York: Basic Books, 1971.

Faunce, William A., "Automation and Leisure," in E. Smigel (ed.), *Work and Leisure: A Contemporary Social Problem*. New Haven, Conn.: College and University Press, 1963.

Feld, Sheila, "Feelings of Adjustment," in F. I. Nye and L. W. Hoffman (eds.), *The Employed Mother in America*. Chicago: Rand McNally, 1963.

Finkelstein, Harry, and Kristine Rosenthal. "Fathering." Research in progress, Brandeis University, Waltham, Mass.

Foltman, Felicia F., *White- and Blue-Collars in a Mill Shutdown*. Ithaca, N.Y.: New York State School of Industrial and Labor Relations, 1968.

French, David, and Elena French, *Working Communally*. New York: Russell Sage Foundation, 1975.

French, J. R. P., Jr., C. J. Tupper, and E. F. Mueller, "Work Loads of University Professors." Cooperative Research Project No. 2171, University of Michigan, 1965.

Freud, Sigmund. *Civilization and Its Discontents*. Trans. by J. Strachey, New York: Norton, 1962.

Frumkin, Robert M., "Occupation and Major Mental Disorders," in A. M. Rose (ed.), *Mental Health and Mental Disorder*. New York: Norton, 1955.

Furstenberg, Frank F., Jr., "The Transmission of Mobility Orientation in the Family." *Social Forces*, 49 (June 1971): 595–603.

Furstenberg, Frank F., Jr., "Work Experience and Family Life," in James O'Toole (ed.), *Work and the Quality of Life: Resource Papers for Work in America*. Cambridge, Mass.: MIT Press, 1974.

Gans, Herbert, *The Urban Villagers: Group and Class in the Life of Italian-Americans*. New York: Free Press, 1962.

Gartner, Allan, and Frank Riessman, "Is There a New Work Ethic?" *American Journal of Orthopsychiatry*, 44 (July 1974): 563–619.

Gecas, Viktor, and F. Ivan Nye, "Sex and Class Differences in Parent-Child Interaction: A Test of Kohn's Hypothesis," *Journal of Marriage and the Family*, 36 (November 1974): 742–9.

Gerstl, Joel E., "Leisure, Taste, and Occupational Milieu," *Social Problems*, 9 (Summer 1961): 56–68.

Gerzon, Mark, *A Childhood for Every Child: The Politics of Parenthood*. New York: Outerbridge and Lazard, 1973.

Gillespie, Dair, "Who Has the Power? The Marital Struggle," *Journal of Marriage and the Family*, 33 (August 1971): 445–58.

Gilman, Charlotte Perkins, *The Home: Its Work and Influence*. New York: McClure, Phillips, 1903.

Gold, Martin, and Carol Slater, "Office, Factory, Store—and Family: A Study of Integration Setting," *American Sociological Review*, 23 (1958): 64–74.

Goldman, Nancy, "The Changing Role of Women in the Armed Forces," *American Journal of Sociology*, 78 (January 1973): 892–911.

Goldthorpe, John H., David Lockwood, Frank Bechhofer, and Jennifer Platt, *The Affluent Worker in the Class Structure*. Cambridge, Eng.: Cambridge University Press, 1969.

Gomberg, William, "Introduction," in A. Shostak and W. Gomberg (eds.), *Blue-Collar World: Studies of the American Worker*. Englewood Cliffs, N.J.: Prentice-Hall, 1964.

Goode, William J., *After Divorce.* Glencoe, Ill.: Free Press, 1956.

Goode, William J., "A Theory of Role Strain," *American Sociological Review,* 25 (August 1960): 483–96.

Goode, William J., "The Theory and Measurement of Family Change," in E. B. Sheldon and W. E. Moore (eds.), *Indicators of Social Change: Concepts and Measurements.* New York: Russell Sage Foundation, 1968.

Goode, William J., *World Revolution and Family Patterns.* New York: Free Press, 1963.

Green, Arnold, "The Middle-Class Male Child and Neurosis," *American Sociological Review,* 11 (February 1946): 31–41.

Greenbaum, Marcia L., *The Shorter Workweek.* Bulletin 50. Ithaca, N.Y.: New York State School of Industrial and Labor Relations, 1962.

Greenberg, Clement, "Work and Leisure under Industrialization," in E. Larrabee and R. Meyersohn (eds.), *Mass Leisure.* Glencoe, Ill.: Free Press, 1958.

Greer, Scott, "Urbanism Reconsidered: A Comparative Study of Local Areas in a Metropolis, *American Sociological Review,* 21 (1956): 19–34.

Gutman, Herbert, "Work, Culture, and Society in Industrializing America, 1819–1918," *American Historical Review,* 77 (June 1973): 531–88.

Haavio-Mannila, Elina, "Satisfaction with Family, Work, Leisure, and Life among Men and Women," *Human Relations,* 24 (December 1971): 585–601.

Hagedorn, Robert, and Sanford Labovitz, "An Analysis of Community and Professional Participation among Occupations," *Social Forces,* 46 (June 1967): 483–91.

Hamilton, Richard F., "The Behavior and Values of Skilled Workers," in A. Shostak and W. Gomberg (eds.), *Blue-Collar World: Studies of the American Worker.* Englewood Cliffs, N.J.: Prentice-Hall, 1964.

Hammond, S. B., "Class and Family," in O. A. Oeser and S. B. Hammond (eds.), *Social Structure and Personality in a City.* London: Routledge and Kegan-Paul, 1954.

Hand, Horace B., "Working Mothers and Maladjusted Children," *Journal of Educational Sociology,* 30 (January 1957): 245–6.

Handel, Gerald, and Lee Rainwater, "Persistence and Change in Working-Class Life Style," in A. Shostak and W. Gomberg (eds.), *Blue-Collar World: Studies of the American Worker.* Englewood Cliffs, N.J., Prentice-Hall, 1964.

Hareven, Tamara, "The Family as Process: The Historical Study of the Family Cycle," *Journal of Social History,* 7 (1974): 322–9.

Hareven, Tamara, "Family Time and Industrial Time: Family and Work in a Planned Corporation Town, 1900–24," *Journal of Urban History,* 1 (May 1975): 365–89.

Hareven, Tamara, "Family Time and Industrial Time: Family and Work 1912–22: The Role of Family and Ethnicity in the Adjustment to Urban Life," *Labor History,* 16 (Spring 1975): 249–65.

Hatt, Paul K., "Occupation and Social Stratification," *American Sociological Review,* 55 (May 1950): 533–43.

Haug, Marie R., "Social Class Measurement and Women's Occupational Roles," *Social Forces,* 52 (1973): 86–98.

Havighurst, Robert J., Paul Hoover Bowman, Gordon P. Liddle, Charles V. Matthews, and James V. Pierce, *Growing Up in River City.* New York: Wiley, 1962.

Havighurst, Robert J., and Allison Davis, "A Comparison of the Chicago and Harvard Studies of Social Class Differences in Child Rearing," *American Sociological Review,* 20 (August 1955): 438–42.

Heckscher, August, and Sebastian de Grazia, "Executive Leisure," *Harvard Business Review,* 37 (July-August 1959): 6–16, 144–56.

Heer, David M., "Dominance and the Working Wife," *Social Forces,* 36 (May 1958): 341–7.

Heer, David M., "The Measurement and Bases of Family Power: An Overview," *Marriage and Family Living,* 25 (May 1963): 133–9.

Henle, Peter, "Recent Growth of Paid Leisure for U.S. Workers," *Monthly Labor Review,* 85 (March 1962): 249–57.

Hennig, Margaret, "Career Development of Women Executives." Ph.D. diss., Harvard Business School, 1970.

Henry, Jules, *Pathways to Madness.* New York: Random House, 1965.

Henry, William E., "The Business Executive: The Psychodynamics of a Social Role," *American Journal of Sociology,* 54 (1949): 286–91.

Hicks, Mary W., and Marilyn Platt, "Marital Happiness and Stability: A Review of the Research in the Sixties," *Journal of Marriage and the Family,* 32 (November 1970): 553–75.

Hochschild, Arlie, "The Role of the Ambassador's Wife: A Preliminary Study," *Journal of Marriage and the Family,* 31 (February 1969): 73–87.

Hoffman, Lois Wladis, "Effects of Maternal Employment on the Child," *Child Development,* 32 (1961): 187–97.

Hoffman, Lois Wladis, "Parental Power Relations and the Division of Household Tasks," *Marriage and Family Living,* 22 (February 1960): 27–35.

Hoffman, Lois Wladis, and F. Ivan Nye, *Working Mothers.* San Francisco: Jossey-Bass, 1974.

Hollingshead, August B., "Class Differences in Family Stability," *The Annals of the American Academy of Political and Social Science,* 272 (November 1950): 39–46.

Hollingshead, August B., *Elmstown's Youth: The Impact of Social Classes on Adolescents.* New York: Wiley, 1958.

Hollingshead, August B., and Frederick C. Redlich, *Social Class and Mental Illness.* New York: Wiley, 1958.

Holmstrom, Linda Lytle, *The Two-Career Family.* Cambridge, Mass.: Schenkman, 1972.

Homans, George C., "Status among Clerical Workers," *Human Organization,* 12 (Spring 1953): 5–10.

House, James S., "The Effects of Occupational Stress on Physical Health," in James O'Toole (ed.), *Work and the Quality of Life.* Cambridge, Mass.: MIT Press, 1974.

Hughes, Everett Cherrington, *Men and Their Work.* Glencoe, Ill.: Free Press, 1958.

Hurvitz, Nathan, "Marital Strain in the Blue-Collar Family," in A. Shostak and W. Gomberg (eds.), *Blue-Collar World: Studies of the American Worker.* Englewood Cliffs, N.J.: Prentice-Hall, 1964.

Inkeles, Alex, "Industrial Man: The Relation of Status to Experience,

Perception, and Value," *American Journal of Sociology*, 66 (July 1960): 1–31.

Inkeles, Alex, "Social Change and Social Character: The Role of Parental Mediation," *Journal of Social Issues*, 11 (1955): 12–23.

Jeffrey, Kirk, "The Family as Utopian Retreat from the City: The Nineteenth Century Contribution," in S. Teselle (ed.), *The Family, Communes, and Utopian Societies*. New York: Harper Torchbooks, 1972.

Kahn, Robert L., and John R. P. French, Jr., "A Summary and Some Tentative Conclusions," *Journal of Social Issues*, 18 (July 1962): 122–9.

Kahne, Hilda, with Andrew I. Kohen, "Economic Perspectives on the Role of Women in the American Economy," *Journal of Economic Literature*, 13 (December 1975): 1249–92.

Kanter, Rosabeth Moss, "Comment VI: Research Styles and Intervention Strategies," *Signs: A Journal of Women in Culture and Society*, 1 (Spring 1976): 282–91. (1976a).

Kanter, Rosabeth Moss, *Commitment and Community*. Cambridge, Mass.: Harvard University Press, 1972. (1972a)

Kanter, Rosabeth Moss, "Commitment and Social Organization: A Study of Commitment Mechanisms in Utopian Communities," *American Sociological Review*, 33 (August 1968): 499–517.

Kanter, Rosabeth Moss, "The Impact of Hierarchical Structures on the Work Behavior of Women and Men," *Social Problems*, 23 (Spring 1976): 415–30. (1976b)

Kanter, Rosabeth Moss, "Intimate Oppression," *Sociological Quarterly*, 15 (Spring 1974): 302–14.

Kanter, Rosabeth Moss, *Men and Women of the Corporation*. New York: Basic Books, 1977.

Kanter, Rosabeth Moss, "The Organization Child: Experience Management in a Nursery School," *Sociology of Education*, 45 (Spring 1972): 186–212. (1972b)

Kanter, Rosabeth Moss, "Women and the Structure of Organizations: Explorations in Theory and Behavior," in M. Millman and R. M. Kanter (eds.), *Another Voice: Feminist Perspectives on Social Life and Social Science*. Garden City, N.Y.: Doubleday Anchor, 1975.

Kanter, Rosabeth Moss (ed.), *Communes: Creating and Managing the Collective Life*. New York: Harper and Row, 1973.

Kanter, Rosabeth Moss, Dennis T. Jaffe, and D. Kelly Weisberg, "Coupling, Parenting, and the Presence of Others," *Family Coordinator*, 24 (October 1975): 433–52.

Kantor, David, and William Lehr, *Inside the Family: Toward a Theory of Family Process*. San Francisco: Jossey-Bass, 1975.

Kasl, Stanislav V., "Work and Mental Health," in James O'Toole (ed.), *Work and the Quality of Life*. Cambridge, Mass.: MIT Press, 1974.

Kasl, Stanislav V., and John R. P. French, Jr., "The Effects of Occupational Status on Physical and Mental Health," *Journal of Social Issues*, 18 (July 1962): 67–89.

Katz, Daniel, and Robert L. Kahn, *Social Psychology of Organizations*. New York: Wiley, 1966.

Katz, Michael, *The Irony of Early School Reform*. Cambridge, Mass.: Harvard University Press, 1968.

Katz, Michael, (ed.), *Class, Bureaucracy, and Schools*. New York: Praeger, 1971.

Kephart, William M., "Occupational Level and Marital Disruption," *American Sociological Review*, 20 (June 1955): 456–65.

Kohn, Melvin L., *Class and Conformity*. Homewood, Ill.: Dorsey Press, 1969.

Kohn, Melvin L., "Social Class and Parent-Child Relationships: An Interpretation," *American Journal of Sociology*, 68 (January 1963): 471–80.

Kohn, Melvin L., "Social Class and Parental Values," *American Journal of Sociology*, 64 (January 1959): 337–51.

Kohn, Melvin L., and Eleanor E. Carroll, "Social Class and the Allocation of Parental Responsibilities," *Sociometry*, 23 (December 1960): 372–92.

Komarovsky, Mirra, "The Voluntary Associations of Urban Dwellers," *American Sociological Review*, 11 (December 1946): 686-98.

Koos, Earl Lomon, *Families in Trouble*. New York: Kings Crown Press, 1946.

Kornhauser, Arthur, "Toward an Assessment of the Mental Health of Factory Workers," *Human Organization*, 21 (Spring 1962): 43–6.

Laing, R. D., and Aaron Esterson, *Sanity, Madness, and the Family*. New York: Basic Books, 1964.

Laslett, Barbara, "The Family as a Public and Private Institution: An Historical Perspective," *Journal of Marriage and the Family*, 35 (August 1973): 480–92.

Lein, Laura, et al., *Work and Family Life*. Final Report to the National Institute of Education, 1974. Cambridge, Mass.: Center for the Study of Public Policy, 1974.

Lenski, Gerhard, "Status Crystallization: A Non-Vertical Dimension of Social Status," *American Sociological Review*, 19 (August 1954): 405–13.

Levinson, Harry, *Emotional Problems in the World of Work*. New York: Harper and Row, 1964.

Levinson, Harry, Charlton R. Price, Kenneth J. Munden, Harold J. Mandl, and Charles M. Solley, *Men, Management, and Mental Health*. Cambridge, Mass.: Harvard University Press, 1962.

Lidz, Theodore, *The Family and Human Adaptation*. New York: International Universities Press, 1963.

Lightfoot, Sara Lawrence, "Family-School Interaction: The Cultural Image of Mothers and Teachers," *Signs: A Journal of Women in Culture and Society*, 2 (Summer 1977): in press.

Lipset, Seymour Martin, and Reinhard Bendix, *Social Mobility in Industrial Society*. Berkeley: University of California Press, 1959.

Lipset, Seymour Martin, Martin Trow, and James Coleman, *Union Democracy*. Glencoe, Ill.: Free Press, 1956.

Locke, Harvey J., and Muriel Mackeprang, "Marital Adjustment and the Employed Wife," *American Journal of Sociology*, 54 (May 1949): 536–8.

Lopata, Helena Z., *Occupation: Housewife*. New York: Oxford University Press, 1971.

Lublin, Joann S., "The Rural Wife," *The Wall Street Journal*, June 2, 1975.

Lundberg, George A., Mirra Komarovsky, and Mary Alice McInerny, *Leisure: A Suburban Study.* New York: Columbia University Press, 1934.

McArthur, Charles, "Personality Differences between Middle and Upper Classes," *Journal of Abnormal and Social Psychology,* 50 (March 1955): 247–54.

McLaughlin, Virginia Yans, "Patterns of Work and Family Organization: Buffalo's Italians," *Journal of Interdisciplinary History,* 2 (Autumn 1971): 299–314.

McLean, Alan A., and Graham C. Taylor, *Mental Health in Industry.* New York: McGraw Hill, 1958.

Maclean, Annie Marion, "Life in the Pennsylvania Coal Fields with Particular Reference to Women," *American Journal of Sociology,* 14 (November 1908): 329–51.

McKinley, Donald Gilbert, *Social Class and Family Life.* New York: Free Press, 1964.

Maccoby, Eleanor E., "Effects upon Children of Their Mothers' Outside Employment," in National Manpower Council, *Work in the Lives of Married Women.* New York: Columbia University Press, 1958.

Maccoby, Michael, and Douglas Carmichael, "Character at Mid-Career," Working Paper, Harvard University Project on Technology, Work, and Character, 1975.

Malec, Michael A., Judith B. Williams, and Edward Z. Dager, "Family Integration, Achievement Values, Academic Self-Concept, and Dropping Out of High School," *Sociological Focus,* 3 (Autumn 1969): 68–77.

"Marrying a Co-worker Becomes Easier at Some Companies," *The Wall Street Journal,* December 2, 1975.

Mayer, Kurt B., *Class and Society.* New York: Random House, 1955.

Mayer, Kurt B., and Sidney Goldstein, "Manual Workers as Small Businessmen," in A. Shostak and W. Gomberg (eds.), *Blue-Collar World: Studies of The American Worker.* Englewood Cliffs, N.J.: Prentice-Hall, 1964.

Meyersohn, Rolf, "Changing Work and Leisure Routines," in E. Smigel (ed.), *Work and Leisure: A Contemporary Social Problem.* New Haven, Conn.: College and University Press, 1963.

Middleton, Russell, and Snell Putney, "Dominance in Decisions in the Family: Race and Class Differences," *American Journal of Sociology,* 65 (1960): 605–9.

Miller, Daniel R., and Guy E. Swanson, *The Changing American Parent.* New York: Wiley, 1958.

Miller, S. M., "The American Lower Classes: A Typological Approach," *Sociology and Social Research,* 48 (April 1964): 281–288. (1964a)

Miller, S. M., "Comparative Social Mobility," *Current Sociology,* 9 (1960): 1–89.

Miller, S. M., "The New Working Class," in A. Shostak and W. Gomberg (eds.), *Blue-Collar World: Studies of the American Worker.* Englewood Cliffs, N.J.: Prentice-Hall, 1964. (1964b)

Miller, S. M., and Frank Reissman, " 'Working-Class Authoritarianism': A Critique of Lipset," *British Journal of Sociology,* 12 (Spring 1961): 263–76.

Miller, S. M., and Frank Reissman, "The Working-Class Subculture: A New View," *Social Problems*, 9 (Summer 1961): 86–97.

Mills, C. Wright, *The Power Elite*. New York: Oxford University Press, 1956.

Mishler, Elliot G., and Nancy E. Waxler, "Family Interaction Processes and Schizophrenia: A Review of Current Theories," *Merrill-Palmer Quarterly of Behavior and Development*, 11 (October 1965): 269–315.

Mizruchi, Ephraim Harold, *Success and Opportunity: A Study of Anomie*. New York: Free Press, 1964.

Monahan, Thomas P., "Divorce by Occupational Level," *Marriage and Family Living*, 17 (November 1955): 322–4.

Monson, Rela Geffen, "Family and Finance: Kin Structures as Facilitators of Articulation with the Economy." Paper presented at the annual meetings of the American Sociological Association, Montreal, August 1974.

Morse, Nancy C., and Robert S. Weiss, "The Function and Meaning of Work and the Job," *American Sociological Review*, 20 (March 1955): 191–8.

Mortimer, Jeylan, Richard Hall, and Reuben Hill, "Husbands' Occupational Attributes as Constraints on Wives' Employment." Paper presented at the annual meetings of the American Sociological Association, New York, August, 1976.

Mott, Paul E., et al., *Shift Work: The Social, Psychological, and Physical Consequences*. Ann Arbor: University of Michigan Press, 1965.

Neel, Robert G., "Nervous Stress in the Industrial Situation," *Personnel Psychology*, 8 (Winter 1955): 405–16.

Nelkin, Dorothy, *On the Season: Aspects of the Migrant Labor System*. Ithaca, N.Y.: New York State School of Industrial and Labor Relations, 1970.

Nelson, Daniel, *Managers and Workers: Origins of the New Factory System in the United States, 1880–1920*. Madison: University of Wisconsin Press, 1975.

Nimkoff, Meyer F., "Occupational Factors and Marriage," *American Journal of Sociology*, 49 (November 1943): 248–54.

Oettinger, Katherine Brownell, "Maternal Employment and Children," in National Manpower Council, *Work in the Lives of Married Women*. New York: Columbia University Press, 1958.

Olsen, Marvin E., "Distribution of Family Responsibilities and Social Stratification," *Marriage and Family Living*, 22 (February 1960): 60–65.

Orden, Susan R., and Norman M. Bradburn, "Dimensions of Marriage Happiness," *American Journal of Sociology*, 73 (November 1968): 715–31.

Orden, Susan R., and Norman M. Bradburn, "Working Wives and Marriage Happiness," *American Journal of Sociology*, 74 (January 1969): 391–407.

Orzack, Louis H., "Work as a 'Central Life Interest' of Professionals," *Social Problems*, 7 (Fall 1959): 125–132.

O'Toole, James (ed.), *Work and the Quality of Life*. Cambridge, Mass.: MIT Press, 1974.

Palmore, Erdman B., and Virginia Stone, "Predictors of Longevity: A

Follow-Up of the Aged in Chapel Hill," *The Gerontologist,* 13 (Spring 1973): 88–90.

Pangurn, Weaver, "The Worker's Leisure and His Individuality," *American Journal of Sociology,* 17 (January 1922): 433–41.

Papenek, Hanna, "Men, Women, and Work: Reflections on the Two-Person Career," *American Journal of Sociology,* 78 (January 1975): 853–72.

Parker, Beulah, *A Mingled Yarn: Chronicle of a Troubled Family.* New Haven: Yale University Press, 1972.

Parker, S. R., "Industry and the Family," *The Sociology of Industry.* New York: Praeger, 1967.

Parsons, Talcott, "The Social Structure of the Family," in R. N. Anshen (ed.), *The Family: Its Function and Destiny.* New York: Harper and Brothers, 1949.

Pearlin, Leonard I., *Class Context and Family Relations: A Cross-National Study.* Boston: Little, Brown, 1970.

Pearlin, Leonard I., "Status Inequality and Stress in Marriage," *American Sociological Review,* 40 (June 1975): 344–57.

Peterson, Evan T., "The Impact of Maternal Employment on the Mother-Daughter Relationship," *Marriage and Family Living,* 23 (November 1961): 355–61.

Pineo, Peter C., "Disenchantment in the Later Years of Marriage," *Marriage and Family Living,* 23 (February 1961): 3–11.

Pleck, Joseph H. "Work and Family Roles: From Sex-Patterned Segregation to Integration." Paper presented at the annual meetings of the American Sociological Association, San Francisco, August 1975.

Poloma, Margaret M., and T. Neal Garland, "The Married Professional Woman: A Study in the Tolerance of Domestication," *Journal of Marriage and the Family,* 33 (August 1971): 531–40.

Price, Charlton R., and Harry Levinson, "Work and Mental Health," in A. Shostak and W. Gomberg (eds.), *Blue-Collar World: Studies of the American Worker.* Englewood Cliffs, N.J.: Prentice-Hall, 1964.

"Profitable Oedipus," *Time,* July 5, 1976: 74.

Purcell, Theodore V., *Blue Collar Man: Patterns of Dual Allegiance in Industry.* Cambridge, Mass.: Harvard University Press, 1960.

Racki, Georg H. E. M., "The Effects of Flexible Working Hours." Ph.D. diss., University of Lausanne, 1975.

Rainwater, Lee, *Behind Ghetto Walls: Black Families in a Federal Slum.* Chicago: Aldine, 1970.

Rainwater, Lee, "Work, Well-being, and Family Life,'" in James O'Toole (ed.), *Work and the Quality of Life.* Cambridge, Mass.: MIT Press, 1974.

Rainwater, Lee, Richard P. Coleman, and Gerald Handel, *Workingman's Wife.* New York: Oceana Publications, 1959.

Rainwater, Lee, and Gerald Handel, "Changing Family Roles in the Working Class," in A. Shostak and W. Gomberg (eds.), *Blue-Collar World: Studies of the American Worker.* Englewood Cliffs, N.J.: Prentice-Hall, 1964.

Rapoport, Robert, "Home and School at the Launch: Some Preliminary Observations," *Oxford Review of Education,* 1 (1975): 277–86. (1975a)

Rapoport, Robert, "The Male's Occupation in Relation to His Decision to Marry," *Acta Sociologica*, 8 (1964): 68–82.

Rapoport, Robert, Personal correspondence, 1975. (1975b)

Rapoport, Robert, and Rhona Rapoport, *Dual-Career Families*. London: Penguin, 1971.

Rapoport, Robert, and Rhona Rapoport, "Work and Family in Contemporary Society," *American Sociological Review*, 30 (June 1965): 381–94.

Rapoport, Robert, Rhona Rapoport, and Victor Thiessen, "Couple Symmetry and Enjoyment," *Journal of Marriage and the Family*, 36 (August 1973): 588–91.

Reiss, David, and Ronald Costell, "Family and Organization: Conflicting and Corresponding Constructions of Reality." Paper presented at the annual meetings of the National Council on Family Relations, 1974.

Renne, Karen S., "Correlates of Dissatisfaction in Marriage," *Journal of Marriage and the Family*, 32 (February 1970): 54–67.

Renshaw, Jean R., "Explorations at the Boundaries of Work and Family Life," Ph.D. diss., University of California at Los Angeles, 1974.

Renshaw, Jean R., "An Exploration of the Dynamics of the Overlapping Worlds of Work and Family," *Family Process*, in press.

Richardson, Anna E., "The Woman Administrator in the Modern Home," *Annals of the American Academy of Political and Social Science*, 143 (May 1929): 21–32.

Richer, Stephen, "The Economics of Child Rearing," *Journal of Marriage and the Family*, 30 (August 1968): 462–6.

Ridley, Carl A., "Exploring the Impact of Work Satisfaction and Involvement on Marital Interaction When Both Partners Are Employed," *Journal of Marriage and the Family*, 35 (May 1973): 229–37.

Riesman, David, "Work and Leisure in Post-Industrial Society," in E. Larrabee and R. Meyersohn (eds.), *Mass Leisure*. Glencoe, Ill.: Free Press, 1958.

Riesman, David, and Warner Bloomberg, Jr., "Work and Leisure: Fusion or Polarity," in C. M. Arensberg, et al. (eds.), *Research in Industrial and Human Relations*. New York: Harper and Brothers, 1957.

Ritter, Kathleen V., and Lowell L. Hargens, "Occupational Positions and Class Identifications of Married Working Women: A Test of the Asymmetry Hypothesis," *American Journal of Sociology*, 80 (January 1975): 934–48.

Rodman, Hyman, "The Lower-Class Value Stretch," *Social Forces*, 42 (December 1963): 205-15

Rodman, Hyman, "Middle-Class Misconceptions about Lower-Class Behavior," in A. Shostak and W. Gomberg (eds.), *Blue-Collar World: Studies of the American Worker*. Englewood Cliffs, N.J.: Prentice-Hall, 1964.

Roe, Anne, *The Psychology of Occupations*. New York: Wiley, 1956.

Rossi, Alice S., "Family Development in a Changing World," *American Journal of Psychiatry*, 128 (March 1972). 47–56.

Safilios-Rothschild, Constantina, "The Influence of the Wife's Degree of Work Commitment upon Some Aspects of Family Organization and

Dynamics," *Journal of Marriage and the Family,* 32 (November 1970): 681–91.

Sales, Stephen M., "Organizational Role as a Risk Factor in Coronary Disease," *Administrative Science Quarterly,* 14 (September 1969): 325–36.

Scanzoni, John H., *Opportunity and the Family: A Study of the Conjugal Family in Relation to the Economic Opportunity Structure.* New York: Free Press, 1970.

Scanzoni, John H., "Resolution of Occupational-Conjugal Role Conflict in Clergy Marriages," *Journal of Marriage and the Family,* 27 (August 1965): 396–402.

Schreiber, E. M., and Nygreen, G. T., "Subjective Social Class in America, 1945–68," *Social Forces,* 48 (March 1970): 348–56.

Seeley, John R., R. Alexander Sim, and E. W. Loosley, *Crestwood Heights: A Study of the Culture of Suburban Life.* Toronto: University of Toronto Press, 1956.

Seeman, Melvin, "On the Personal Consequences of Alienation in Work," *American Sociological Review,* 32 (April 1967): 273–85.

Segal, David R., and Marcus Felson, "Social Stratification and Family Economic Behavior," in E. B. Sheldon (ed), *Family Economic Behavior.* Philadelphia: Lippincott, 1973.

Seidenberg, Robert, *Corporate Wives—Corporate Casualties?* New York: AMACOM, 1973.

Sennett, Richard, and Jonathan Cobb, *The Hidden Injuries of Class.* New York: Knopf, 1972.

Sexton, Patricia Cayo, "Wife of the 'Happy Worker'," in A. Shostak and W. Gomberg (eds.), *Blue-Collar World: Studies of the American Worker.* Englewood Cliffs, N.J.: Prentice-Hall, 1964.

Siegel, Alberta Envall, Lois Meek Stolz, Ethel Alice Hitchcock, and Jean Adamson, "Dependence and Independence in the Children of Working Mothers," *Child Development,* 30 (December 1959): 533–46.

Skolnick, Arlene, "The Family Revisited: Themes in Recent Social Science Research," *Journal of Interdisciplinary History,* 5 (Spring 1975): 703–19.

Slater, Philip, "Parental Role Differentiation," *American Journal of Sociology,* 67 (November 1961): 296–311.

Smelser, Neil J., *Social Change in the Industrial Revolution: An Application of Theory to the British Cotton Industry.* Chicago: University of Chicago Press, 1959.

Smigel, Erwin O., "Introduction," in *Work and Leisure: A Contemporary Social Problem.* New Haven: College and University Press, 1963.

Smith, Lucinda, "Night Work: Another Lifestyle," *Boston Sunday Globe,* November 24, 1974, pp. A8, A12.

Stein, Barry A., Allan Cohen, and Herman Gadon, "Flextime: Work When You Want to," *Psychology Today,* 10 (June 1976): 40–3, 80.

Stein, Barry A., and Rosabeth Moss Kanter, "From Family to Business: The Evolution of a Small Company." Manuscript in progress, Center for Social and Evaluation Research, University of Massachusetts, Boston.

Steiner, Jerome, "What Price Success?" *Harvard Business Review* (March-April 1972): 69–74.

Steinmetz, Suzanne K., "Occupational Environment in Relation to Physical Punishment and Dogmatism," in S. Steinmetz and M. Strauss (eds.), *Violence in the Family.* New York: Dodd, Mead, 1974.

Stessin, Lawrence, "Fixing the Liability for Work Pressures," *The New York Times*, April 25, 1976: III, 3:1.

Stevens, William K., "If Recession Comes in the Door, Love May Fly out the Window," *The New York Times*, July 28, 1975: 17.

Stolz, Lois Meek, "Effects of Maternal Employment on Children: Evidence from Research," *Child Development*, 31 (December 1960): 749–82.

Stouffer, Samuel A., and Paul S. Lazarsfeld, "Research Memorandum on the Family in the Depression," *Social Science Research Council Bulletin*, 29 (1937).

Straus, Murray A., "The Role of the Wife in the Settlement of the Columbia Basin Project," *Marriage and Family Living*, 20 (February 1958): 59–64.

Swados, Harvey, "Less Work–Less Leisure," *The Nation*, 186 (February 22, 1958): 153–8.

Swados, Harvey, *On the Line.* Boston: Little, Brown, 1957.

Tallman, Irving, and Ramona Morgner, "Life-Style Differences among Urban and Suburban Blue-Collar Families," *Social Forces*, 48 (March 1970): 334–48.

Titmuss, Richard M., *Essays on "The Welfare State."* Boston: Beacon Press, 1969. (First published, 1958.)

Torbert, William R., with Malcolm P. Rogers, *Being for the Most Part Puppets: The Interaction of Men's Labor, Leisure, and Politics.* Cambridge, Mass.: Shenckman, 1973.

Turner, Ralph H., *The Social Context of Ambition.* San Francisco: Chandler, 1964.

Turner, Ralph H., "Some Family Determinants of Ambition," *Sociology and Social Research*, 46 (July 1962): 397–411.

Udry, J. Richard, "Marital Instability by Race, Sex, Education, and Occupation Using 1960 Census Data," *American Journal of Sociology*, 72 (September 1966): 203–9.

Udry, J. Richard, *The Social Context of Marriage.* Philadelphia: Lippincott, 1966.

Veroff, Joseph, and Sheila Feld, *Marriage and Work in America.* New York: Van Nostrand-Reinhold, 1970.

Vogel, Ezra F., and Norman W. Bell, "The Emotionally Disturbed Child as Family Scapegoat," in G. Handel (ed.), *The Psychosocial Interior of the Family.* Chicago: Aldine, 1967.

Vogel, Lise, "Women of Spirit, Women of Action: Mill Workers of Nineteenth Century New England." Unpublished paper, Brandeis University, Waltham, Mass., 1975.

Wade, Michael, *Flexible Working Hours in Practice.* New York: Wiley (Halsted Press), 1973.

Warner, W. Lloyd, and James C. Abegglen, *Big Business Leaders in America.* New York: Harper and Brothers, 1955.

Warner, W. Lloyd, and James C. Abegglen, "Successful Wives of Successful Executives," *Harvard Business Review*, 44 (March-April 1956): 64–70.

Warren, Rachelle Barcus, "The Work Role and Problem Coping: Sex Differentials in the Use of Helping Systems in Urban Communities." Paper presented at the annual meetings of the American Sociological Association, San Francisco, August 1975.

Weatherly, U. G., "How Does the Access of Women to Industrial Occupations React on the Family?" *American Journal of Sociology,* 14 (May 1909): 740–65.

Weber, Max, *The Theory of Social and Economic Organization.* A. Henderson and T. Parsons, trans. New York: Oxford University Press, 1947.

Weeks, H. Ashley, "Differential Divorce Rates by Occupations," *Social Forces,* 21 (March 1942-3): 344–7.

Weil, Mildred W., "An Analysis of the Factors Influencing Married Women's Actual or Planned Work Force Participation," *American Sociological Review,* 26 (January 1961): 91–6.

Weiss, Robert S., and David Riesman, "Some Issues in the Future of Leisure," *Social Problems,* 9 (Summer 1961): 78–86.

Weissman, Myrna M., and Eugene S. Paykel, *The Depressed Woman: A Study of Social Relationships.* Chicago: University of Chicago Press, 1974.

Weissman, Myrna M., and Eugene S. Paykel, "Moving and Depression in Women," *Society,* 9 (July-August 1972): 24–8.

White, R. Clyde, "Social Class Differences in the Uses of Leisure," *American Journal of Sociology,* 61 (September 1955): 145–50.

Whyte, William H., Jr., "The Wife Problem," *Life* (January 7, 1952): 32–48.

Whyte, William H., Jr., "The Wives of Management," *Fortune* (October 1951): 86–8, 204–13; (November 1951): 109–11, 150–8.

Wilensky, Harold L., "Orderly Careers and Social Participation: The Impact of Work History on Social Integration in the Middle Mass," *American Sociological Review,* 26 (August 1961): 521–39.

Wilensky, Harold L., "The Uneven Distribution of Leisure: The Impact of Economic Growth on 'Free Time'," *Social Problems,* 9 (Summer 1961): 107–45.

Wilensky, Harold L., "Work as a Social Problem," in H. S. Becker (ed.), *Social Problems: A Modern Approach.* New York: Wiley, 1966.

Wilensky, Harold L., "Work, Careers, and Social Integration," *International Social Science Journal,* 12 (1960): 543–60.

Wilensky, Harold L., and Hugh Edwards, "The Skidder: Ideological Adjustments of Downward Mobile Workers," *American Sociological Review,* 24 (April 1959): 215–31.

Williams, Judith, E. Z. Dager, and Michael A. Malec, "Social Class, Ethnicity, and Adolescent Identification with Parents." Paper presented at the annual meetings of the American Sociological Association, New Orleans, August 1972.

Williamson, Robert C., "Economic Factors in Marital Adjustment," *Marriage and Family Living,* 14 (November 1952): 298–301.

Williamson, Robert, C., "Socio-economic Factors and Marital Adjustment in an Urban Setting," *American Sociological Review,* 19 (April 1954): 213–6.

Willmott, Peter, "Family, Work and Leisure Conflicts among Male Employees: Some Preliminary Findings," *Human Relations,* 24 (December 1971): 575–84.

Wilson, Alan B., "Residential Segregation of Social Classes and Aspirations of High School Boys," *American Sociological Review,* 24 (October 1959): 836–45.

Witt, Matt, "It's in Our Blood: Three Generations of a Coal Mining Family," *United Mine Workers Journal,* 86 (September 1975): 8–17.

Wolfe, Donald M., and J. Diedrick Snoek, "A Study of Tensions and Adjustments under Role Conflict," *Journal of Social Issues,* 18 (July 1962): 102–21.

Wright, Charles R., and Herbert H. Hyman, "Voluntary Association Memberships of American Adults," *American Sociological Review,* 23 (June 1958): 284–94.

Wynne, Lyman C., Irving M. Ryckoff, Juliana Day, and Stanley I. Hirsch, "Pseudo-mutuality in the Family Relations of Schizophrenics," *Psychiatry,* 21 (1958): 205–20.

Young, Michael, and Peter Willmott, *The Symmetrical Family.* New York: Pantheon, 1973.

Zablocki, Benjamin, *The Joyful Community.* Baltimore: Penguin, 1971.

Zablocki, Benjamin, and Rosabeth Moss Kanter, "Differentiation of Life Styles," *Annual Review of Sociology,* 2 (1976): 269–98.

Zeisel, Joseph S., "The Workweek in American Industry, 1850-1956," *Monthly Labor Review,* 81 (January 1958): 23–9.

Zeitlin, Maurice, "Corporate Ownership and Control: The Large Corporation and the Capitalist Class," *American Journal of Sociology,* 79 (March 1974): 1073–1119.

Zunich, Michael, "Lower-class Mothers' Behavior and Attitudes toward Child Rearing," *Psychological Reports,* 19 (December 1971): 1051–8.